THE GREAT AWAKENING

IGNITING REGIONAL REVIVAL

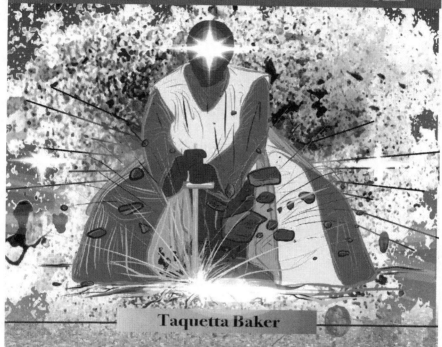

Taquetta Baker

Book Synopsis

*"**The Great Awakening - Igniting Regional Revival**," poses a SHIFTING perspective regarding revival. Though important, this book, is not about re-digging revival wells, re-sparking old works of revivalists, having continual services and then when Pentecost comes, quenching it by ending the services as fast as they started. This book is about understanding that we are to live a life of revival. That people, churches, and ministries are to be the very ignited revival of God in communities, regions, and nations. That fivefold ministry was given to the body of Christ to train, equip, and release saints and ministries to live and minister through revival fire as Jesus died so we could live in resurrection power and in continual daily newness.*

As we SHIFTED to an eternal dwelling through salvation, our fire was to never be quenched. We the people of God - the ministries of God - are revival. That reformation is intertwined in revival and without reformation, revival cannot sustain. That we must displace principalities and powers and war and contend with demonic forces to live inside daily revival. Once we grasp this revelation, we can use the strategies in this book to truly awaken revival within us, families, ministries, businesses, climates, atmospheres, and communities, such that we awaken to regional revival that burns eternally for Jesus, while establishing his fame and kingdom all over the universe.

TaquettaBaker@Kingdomshifters.com
(Website) Kingdomshifters.com
Connect with Taquetta via Facebook or YouTube

Taquetta's Bio

Taquetta Baker is the founder of Kingdom Shifters Ministries (KSM). She has authored fourteen books and two decree CD's. Taquetta has a Master's Degree in Community Counseling with an emphasis on Marriage, Children and Family Counseling, a Bachelor's Degree in Psychology and Associates Degree in Business Administration. In addition, Taquetta has a Therapon Belief Therapist Certification from Therapon Institute and has 22 years of professional and Christian Counseling experience.

Taquetta is also gifted at empowering and assisting people with launching ministries, businesses and books and provides mentoring, counseling and vision casting through Kingdom Shifters Kingdom Wellness Program. Taquetta serves on the Board of Directors for New Day Community Ministries, Inc. of Muncie, IN. In October 2008, Taquetta graduated from the Eagles Dance Institute under Dr. Pamela Hardy and received her license in the area of liturgical dance. Before launching into her own ministry, Taquetta served at her previous church for 12 years. She was a prophet, pioneer and leader of Shekinah Expressions Dance Ministry, teacher, member of the presbytery board, and overseer of the Altar Workers Ministry. Taquetta receives mentoring and ministry covering from Bishop Jackie Green, Founder of JGM-National PrayerLife Institute (Phoenix, AZ), and was ordained as an Apostle on June 7, 2014.

Taquetta flows through the wells of warfare and worship and mantles an apostolic mandate of judging and establishing God's kingdom in people, ministries, communities, and regions. Taquetta travels in foreign missions and throughout the United States. She has mentored and established dance, altar workers, deliverance, and prophetic ministries. Taquetta ministers in the areas of fine arts, all manners of prayer, fivefold ministry, deliverance, healing, miracles, atmospheric worship, and empowers and train people in their destiny and life's vision.

Connect with Taquetta and KSM at <u>kingdomshifters.com</u> or via Facebook.

Table of Contents

FORWARD
From Bishop Dr. Jackie L. Green

In 1994, I was blessed to travel to Argentina during a time of a Great Awakening and a tremendous revival that lasted for over ten years. It was evident that the Holy Spirit was orchestrating the thousands of salvations, church growth, child evangelism, miracles, signs, and wonders. It had been a result of years and years of intercession and tears and the pastors (gatekeepers) coming together to cry out to God for a visitation in their land. **There is no substitute for a GREAT MOVE OF GOD... A GREAT AWAKENING... TO SHAKE AND SAVE A PEOPLE OR A NATION.**

When I read this book **THE GREAT AWAKENING, IGNITING REGIONAL REVIVAL BY APOSTLE TAQUETTA BAKER,** *I could see how God is going to use this book and use her to ignite such an awakening in our regions and nation. Great Awakenings are orchestrated sometimes 50 to 100 years a part. Apostle Baker is concise and clear on how to prepare for such a much needed great awakening in your regions. True awakenings affects the churched and unchurched like nothing else.*

This book is a training tool to raise up regional revivalist, teaching them to cultivate walking by faith in the supernatural and recognizing and overcoming the attacks against revivalist. **Thwarting Attacks Against Revivalist** *is a most profound chapter defining satanic attacks against revival movements and the revivalists. This book also is getting the Church ready for what will be required when a Great Awakening comes. It will require training, equipping, laboring, vision, and birthing forth the strategies of God before and after a GREAT MOVE OF GOD!*

"The Region Knows My Name" *chapter is a personal call to not only knowing your region, but making sure you have been sent to that region, and understand the power you have to speak to your* *region in the Spirit and command respect and heavenly back up. The author makes sure that the Gatekeepers in the region clearly understand their role in intercession which ignites revival in a region. The Gatekeepers determine access or deny access in the region as they guard against anything that could enter the region and disrupt God's purposes.*

*Finally, let me say the future of the Church is good hands. Apostle Taquetta is a young apostle and a strong representative of the Millennial generation that walks in the authority of Christ and has a vision and heart for a GREAT AWAKENING. We must not underestimate whom God will use to usher in this GREAT AWAKENING, and for sure it is usually those we least expect. Thank God, the author has an ear to hear what the Spirit is saying and is **"awake, alert, and available"** to help the Body of Christ usher in personal, church, city, regional, state, national, and global revival.*

Mine Eyes have seen the Glory of Revival South America... and I want to live to see a GREAT AWAKENING in the United States in our cities, national regions and in the White House (our seat of government) in the 21st Century.

I say, "Go forward" igniting regional revival... it must happen, and it will happen!

Blessings,
Bishop Dr. Jackie L. Green
JGM International Prayer Life Institute
Redlands, CA

For more information regarding Bishop Jackie Green at Jgmenternational.org.

REVIVAL! THE GREAT AWAKENING

Revival consists of restoring our lives, families, and regions to the original state God intended us to live before the fall of man in the Garden of Eden, and after Jesus came to redeem us to eternal life. You see, it was always God's desire for man to be blessed and to prosper.

> *Genesis 1:28 And God blessed them, and God said unto them, Be fruitful, and multiply, and replenish the earth, and subdue it: and have dominion over the fish of the sea, and over the fowl of the air, and over every living thing that moveth upon the earth.*

God's mandate for man to live successfully in the earth never changes. It was man's choices that altered the path for bringing that mandate to pass. God has continuously sought to restore covenant relationship and revive man unto eternal life. Therefore, revival is not a new concept or a fleeting concept.

> *Ecclesiastes 1:8 What has been will be again, what has been done will be done again; there is nothing new under the sun.*

Revival is an evolving concept. As man and the earth evolves, we will always see the continual need for revival and reformation. Though restoration of health, liberty, wealth, purity, etc., will occur, the focus of restoration should not be for earthly prosperity, but restoration unto eternal life and the original prosperity that God intended for man and the earth. Many people do not view revival as a part of their daily walk with God, God will quicken individuals with a fire to ignite revival in bodies of people, communities, regions, and nations. We must grasp the understanding that the revival fire should never go out.

1

- ✓ This should not be a seasonal experience.
- ✓ This should not be a series of services where God moves then the move is gone.
- ✓ This should not be an effort to restore people, ministries, or communities to a time where God's presence was strong and evident.
- ✓ This should not be for a select few, while others die in their sins, sickness, and transgressions.

This should be a Holy Ghost fire with Jesus as the chief cornerstone so that we build the kingdom of God upon it. A lasting kingdom that has solid dominion in the earth. A kingdom that can endure and sustain the lineage of Jesus Christ and his sovereign reign, from generation to generation.

> *Psalms 135:13 Thy kingdom is an everlasting kingdom, and thy dominion endureth throughout all generations.*

> *1Timothy 1:14-17 And the grace of our Lord was exceeding abundant with faith and love which is in Christ Jesus. This is a faithful saying, and worthy of all acceptation, that Christ Jesus came into the world to save sinners; of whom I am chief. Howbeit for this cause I obtained mercy, that in me first Jesus Christ might shew forth all longsuffering, for a pattern to them which should hereafter believe on him to life everlasting. Now unto the King eternal, immortal, invisible, the only wise God, be honour and glory for ever and ever. Amen.*

If we are going to experience true Godly revival where people, regions, and nations burn for Jesus, it is pertinent to SHIFT our mindsets of thinking revival is just an experience or event, as this quenches revival. In addition, we must be willing to do the work of building an eternal fire. Revival will never occur in our:

- Comfort zones
- Little time frames
- Religious quirks and hang ups
- Manmade and self-absorbed agendas
- Murmuring and complaining
- Divisive mindsets where we tear down the very people and kingdom we are claiming to save, establish, empower, and build
- Safe four corner churches, ministries, and online platforms, while never going outside of the four walls of our buildings, and only ministering in atmospheric dimensions
- Religious doctrine where we only pray for revival, but never physically train, equip, and release saints to infiltrate communities and establish the kingdom of God in the earth

I hear people contending we do not need revival when Jesus was calling himself the resurrection even before he died for our sins.

> *John 11:25-26. Jesus said to her, I am the resurrection and the life; he who believes in Me will live even if he dies, and everyone who lives and believes in Me will never die. Do you believe this?*

Jesus came to revive us unto eternal life.

> *John 3:16 For God so loved the world that he gave his one and only Son, that whoever believes in him shall not perish but have eternal life.*

After Jesus fulfilled his purpose, he rose with governmental power over everything. He was revival! SHIFT! He wanted the entire world to be awakened and living through his redemptive authority.

Matthew 28:16-18 Then the eleven disciples went away into Galilee, into a mountain where Jesus had appointed them. And when they saw him, they worshipped him: but some doubted. And Jesus came and spake unto them, saying, All power is given unto me in heaven and in earth. Go ye therefore, and teach all nations, baptizing them in the name of the Father, and of the Son, and of the Holy Ghost: Teaching them to observe all things whatsoever I have commanded you: and, lo, I am with you alway, even unto the end of the world. Amen.

REVIVAL DEMARCATION DECREE

Decree these demarcations over your life consistently to awaken revival fire!

As Revival Awakens In Me, I Will:

Awaken	Enliven	Recapture	Reinstitute	Resurrect
Make Alive	Invigorate	Reclaim	Reestablish	Regenerate
Make Eternal	Quicken	Redeem	Reintroduce	Rekindle
Bring back	Renew	Reintroduce	Revitalize	Reinvigorate
Energize	Reactivate	Resuscitate	Refresh	Reanimate
Revivify	Regenerate	Rejuvenate	Strengthen	Stimulate

Through Me, There Will Be

A Fresh awakening, a divine awakening, a great awakening.

Restoration of life, consciousness, inheritance, kingly rights.

Revival of destiny, purpose, establishment of the kingdom.

For I Will

Make operative or valid again.
Bring back into notice, use, or currency.
Bring around, bring back to consciousness regain life, or strength.
Give new strength, energy, zeal, or power.
Restore interest in, recognition, or the popularity of.
Establish redemption.
Establish the God given eternity of a person, place, thing, matter.
Make operative or valid again.
This Is My Mandate As A Mantled Revivalist!

PERSONAL REVIVAL

One day I received a word of revelation from a prophet that there were flames on the bottom of my feet. I received this word several more times as I begin to really align with destiny and walk in the word God had given me that my ministry would restore revival in my region. At the time, I did not know what these visions meant, but now I know it as revival fire.

If God chooses you to ignite revival, he will first birth revival in you. I believe this equips you to:

- ✓ Be revival
- ✓ Be the example of revival
- ✓ Carry revival everywhere you go

Joshua 1:3 *Now after the death of Moses the servant of the Lord it came to pass, that the Lord spake unto Joshua the son of Nun, Moses' minister, saying, Moses my servant is dead; now therefore arise, go over this Jordan, thou, and all this people, unto the land which I do give to them, even to the children of Israel. Every place that the sole of your foot shall tread upon, that have I given unto you, as I said unto Moses.*

Death had come to Moses, but God's vision and promises were yet alive. Moses was revival for the Israelites. God was now quickening Joshua to be revival so that the Israelites would still believe in the promises and vision of God for their lives, families, and generations. Joshua was not just revival among the Israelites, but every place the soles of his feet tread. He was revival that trampled down darkness while igniting and establishing the kingdom of God in his midst.

Revival starts with a personal awakening within people who want the fullness of salvation manifested in every area of their lives. Revivalist recognize that they can have the kingdom of God RIGHT NOW - in its fullness - and understands that the fullness of salvation is now. It is not something to be attained but seized.

> *Philippians* **3:12-14** *The New King James Bible Not that I have already attained, or am already perfected; but I press on, that I may lay hold of that for which Christ Jesus has also laid hold of me. Brethren, I do not count myself to have apprehended; but one thing I do, forgetting those things which are behind and reaching forward to those things which are ahead, I press toward the goal for the prize of the upward call of God in Christ Jesus.*

> **Verse 12-16 The Message Bible** *I'm not saying that I have this all together, that I have it made. But I am well on my way, reaching out for Christ, who has so wondrously reached out for me. Friends, don't get me wrong: By no means do I count myself an expert in all of this, but I've got my eye on the goal, where God is beckoning us onward – to Jesus. I'm off and running, and I'm not turning back.*

> *So let's keep focused on that goal, those of us who want everything God has for us. If any of you have something else in mind, something less than total commitment, God will clear your blurred vision – you'll see it yet! Now that we're on the right track, let's stay on it.*

Revivalists are seeking to lay claim to the inheritance that God has given them and the body of Christ. They reject measure. They reject giving God a measure of themselves and reject having only a measure of God. For this reason, revivalists are mantled to lay siege of the promises of God in their personal lives, families, lineages, regions, and nations.

Many people have a passion for revival, but not the birthing mantle of true revival. Though not always the case, this is the reason we have seen sparks and movements of revival, but not a consistent eternal burning of revival.

Passion is great, but revival cannot be birthed through the emotions or feelings. It has to be birthed through the spirit, otherwise passion burns out. When emotional passion quenches, so does revival and the strength and motivation to continue plowing and contending for revival.

When you have spiritual passion, you possess:

Obedience
1Kings 8:58 New International Bible May he turn our hearts to him, to walk in <u>obedience</u> to him…

Commitment
1Kings 8:61 New International Bible And may your hearts be fully committed to the LORD our God, to live by his decrees and obey his commands, as at this time.

Consistency
Acts 1:3 He presented himself alive to them after his suffering by many proofs, appearing to them during forty days and speaking about the kingdom of God.

Godly Focus
Colossians 3:23 And whatsoever ye do, do [it] heartily, as to the Lord, and not unto men.

Discipline
1Corinthians 9:24-26a New Living Bible Don't you realize that in a race everyone runs, but only one person gets the prize? So run to win! All athletes are disciplined in their training. They do it to win a prize that will fade away,

but we do it for an eternal prize. So I run with purpose in every step.

Zeal
Romans 12:10-11 NIV Be devoted to one another in love. Honor one another above yourselves. Never be lacking in zeal, but keep your spiritual fervor, serving the Lord.

Dead To Sin
Galatians 5:24 And they that are Christ's have crucified the flesh with the affections and lusts.

Godly Cravings
Psalms 84:2 My soul longeth, yea, even fainteth for the courts of the LORD: my heart and my flesh crieth out for the living God.

Psalms 63:1 (A Psalm of David, when he was in the wilderness of Judah.) O God, thou [art] my God; early will I seek thee: my soul thirsteth for thee, my flesh longeth for thee in a dry and thirsty land, where no water is.

God Lead
Psalms 32:8 I will instruct thee and teach thee in the way which thou shalt go: I will guide thee with mine eye.

Greater Works
John 14:12 Verily, verily, I say unto you, He that believeth on me, the works that I do shall he do also; and greater [works] than these shall he do; because I go unto my Father.

Godly Establishment
Psalm 90:17 New International Bible May the favor of the Lord our God rest on us; establish the work of our hands for us – yes, establish the work of our hands.

Godly passion grounds you in the vision and purpose of God, and empowers you with the fruit to bring revival to pass.

Another essential key we need to grasp regarding revival is that it is not just a movement we are striving to ignite, it is a lifestyle of living inside and through the eternal, unquenchable fire of God.

> **Romans 12:11** *The Amplified Bible Never lag in zeal and in earnest endeavor; be aglow and burning with the Spirit, serving the Lord.*

> **New International Revision Bible** *Never let the fire in your heart go out. Keep it alive. Serve the Lord.*

If we lived a life of revival, we would always live in pursuit of God's burning fire, while posturing ourselves for continual awakening, refreshing, enlightenment, empowerment, and re-strengthening to be ever burning in the work of the Lord.

Fire has the potential to spread quickly and spark a blaze in that which it seizes. It has the potential to destroy or refine that which it ignites. The *flame* is the visible portion of the fire. It is what you cannot see that determines if the flame continues to burn – radiating an eternal revival fire.

Mantle of Revival:

> **Isaiah 59:16-17 The Amplified Bible** *And He saw that there was no man and wondered that there was no intercessor [no one to intervene on behalf of truth and right]; therefore His own arm brought Him victory, and His own righteousness [having the Spirit without measure] sustained Him. For [the Lord] put on righteousness as a*

breastplate or coat of mail, and salvation as a helmet upon His head; He put on garments of vengeance for clothing and was clad with zeal [and furious divine jealousy] as a cloak.

When you are mantled with revival, you are an armored intercessor ordained by God to restore victory, righteousness, salvation, and the limitless Holy Spirit of God to people, families, regions, and nations. Your very life is the:

- Entreatment for revival (intercession)
- Stirring for revival (intercession)
- Contending and hearing for revival (warfare)
- Vengeance for revival (judgement and justice)
- Holiness, purity, and virtue for revival (righteousness)
- Fruit of revival (salvation)
- Protector and covering of revival (mantled garment of vengeance and zeal)
- Radiance of revival (mantled garment of vengeance and zeal)
- Wellness of revival (salvation)
- Zealous heart of God for revival (Godly jealousy)
- Reality of revival (victory)
- Holy Spirit fire of revival (Holy Spirit without measure)

It will blaze in everything you do and will ignite the flame of God everywhere you go.

It will judge and kill things that need to die and raise and revive things that need to live.

It will enrage and judge devils and wreak vengeance on wickedness.

It will draw the lost to salvation and restore the backslider to Godly destiny.

It will SHIFT religious hearts and systems into the liberated Holy Spirit of God and posture them at the foot of Jesus.

It will restore prosperity to people, families, the lands, and regions, making salvation evident to the believing and unbelieving.

It will make regions and nations of people proclaim his name - making him famous all down through the generations.

Decreeing that if God has called you to ignite revival, you are accepting your calling as his mantle is awakening revival fire within, upon, and all around you. Everywhere the souls of your feet tread. **REVIVAL! SHIFT!**

PURPOSE OF REGIONAL REVIVAL

The purpose of regional revival is to restore reformation while rebuilding and reestablishing people, lands, atmospheres, climates, and regions in the fullness of salvation. The essential mandate of churches and fivefold ministry is to be an edifice for reigning and governing God's kingdom and revival fire in the earth, such that salvation reigns in the earth.

> *Ephesians 4:11-13 The Amplified Bible And His gifts were [varied; He Himself appointed and gave men to us] some to be apostles (special messengers), some prophets (inspired preachers and expounders), some evangelists (preachers of the Gospel, traveling missionaries), some pastors (shepherds of His flock) and teachers. His intention was the perfecting and the full equipping of the saints (His consecrated people), [that they should do] the work of ministering toward building up Christ's body (the church), [That it might develop] until we all attain oneness in the faith and in the comprehension of the [full and accurate] knowledge of the Son of God, that [we might arrive] at really mature manhood (the completeness of personality which is nothing less than the standard height of Christ's own perfection), the measure of the stature of the fullness of the Christ and the completeness found in Him.*

God gave these gifts after he resurrected, taking authority over and death and hell.

> *Verse 8-10 The Amplified Bible Therefore it is said, When He ascended on high, He led captivity captive [He led a train of vanquished foes] and He bestowed gifts on men. [But He ascended?] Now what can this, He ascended, mean but that He had previously descended from [the heights of] heaven into [the depths], the lower parts of the earth? He*

14

Who descended is the [very] same as He Who also has ascended high above all the heavens, that He [His presence] might fill all things (the whole universe, from the lowest to the highest).

Jesus wanted to make it was clear that we were living from an eternal perspective, and that death and devils no longer ruled us. We had been awakened by eternal revival fire, for revival is an eternal perspective. It is the divine understanding that though our outward man is perishing, our inner man is being renewed day by day.

> *2Corinthians 4:16 The Amplified Bible Therefore we do not become discouraged (utterly spiritless, exhausted, and wearied out through fear). Though our outer man is [progressively] decaying and wasting away, yet our inner self is being [progressively] renewed day after day. For our light, momentary affliction (this slight distress of the passing hour) is ever more and more abundantly preparing and producing and achieving for us an everlasting weight of glory [beyond all measure, excessively surpassing all comparisons and all calculations, a vast and transcendent glory and blessedness never to cease!].*

COME ON! THAT IS REVIVAL!

The revival fire of God was to never go out. Jesus resurrected to reestablish renewed daily life in people, lands, and regions. He equipped the body of Christ with governmental fivefold ministry to ensure that his kingdom reigned and burned in the earth. Somewhere along the way, fivefold ministry became obsolete and replaced with a one-man pastoral system. As fivefold ministry is being restored to the body of Christ, it has become more about titles, conferences, prophetic words, personal kingdoms, and personal advancement, than truly governing regions and

15

equipping the saints to carry the fire to their region, such that we save the lost, heal the sick, raise the dead, and freely impart revival fire into those in our sphere of influence. Such that we become a catalyst in communities and regions for health, wealth, provision, caring for the needy, destiny development, advancement, fellowship, guidance, counsel, morals, and standards. We must SHIFT back to this original intent to reclaim God's name, will, purpose, and kingdom reign in the earth.

This revival perspective did not just manifest when Jesus came and died. Before the fall of man, God's kingdom and purpose reigned in the earth and Adam and Eve lived through the "*Ruah*" breath of God, as God made the earth and everything in it, through his Spirit which is eternal in nature.

> *Genesis 1:1-2 In the beginning God created the heaven and the earth. And the earth was without form, and void; and darkness was upon the face of the deep. And the Spirit of God moved upon the face of the waters.*

God is an eternal God, and his Spirit bears his eternal existence. Adam and Eve lived through God's eternal Spirit - thus known as revival, as revival denotes continual living and newness of life. Isn't it great pondering that God is always reviving, therefore we were never to die? We were to constantly be revived, renewed, and reigning in life through this disposition.

> *Genesis 1:26-31 And God said, Let us make man in our image, after our likeness: and let them have dominion over the fish of the sea, and over the fowl of the air, and over the cattle, and over all the earth, and over every creeping thing that creepeth upon the earth. So God created man in his own image, in the image of God created he him; male and*

female created he them. And God blessed them, and God said unto them, Be fruitful, and multiply, and replenish the earth, and subdue it: and have dominion over the fish of the sea, and over the fowl of the air, and over every living thing that moveth upon the earth.

And God said, Behold, I have given you every herb bearing seed, which is upon the face of all the earth, and every tree, in the which is the fruit of a tree yielding seed; to you it shall be for meat. And to every beast of the earth, and to every fowl of the air, and to every thing that creepeth upon the earth, wherein there is life, I have given every green herb for meat: and it was so. And God saw every thing that he had made, and, behold, it was very good. And the evening and the morning were the sixth day.

As Adam and Eve lived in the garden they lived through an eternal state; nothing was perishing. Not until sin entered the world. Sin snuffed out revival. It snuffed out eternal life. Jesus restored revival. After Jesus ascended into heaven, the apostles begin to establish revival in the earth. Many ministries they planted within communities and regions, manifested revival. They had the manifested glory of salvation and resurrection of the cross upon them, where it was evident that Jesus reigned there. As we study the New Testament, we can discern which ministries and regions rejected Jesus or only embraced a measure of salvation, because they did not possess the fullness of revival. *Acts 2:31-47* is an example of a ministry and community that possessed revival fire.

He seeing this before spake of the resurrection of Christ, that his soul was not left in hell, neither his flesh did see corruption. This Jesus hath God raised up, whereof we all are witnesses. Therefore being by the right hand of God exalted, and having received of the Father the promise of the

Holy Ghost, he hath shed forth this, which ye now see and hear. For David is not ascended into the heavens: but he saith himself, The Lord said unto my Lord, Sit thou on my right hand, Until I make thy foes thy footstool. Therefore let all the house of Israel know assuredly, that God hath made that same Jesus, whom ye have crucified, both Lord and Christ.

Now when they heard this, they were pricked in their heart, and said unto Peter and to the rest of the apostles, Men and brethren, what shall we do? Then Peter said unto them, Repent, and be baptized every one of you in the name of Jesus Christ for the remission of sins, and ye shall receive the gift of the Holy Ghost. For the promise is unto you, and to your children, and to all that are afar off, even as many as the Lord our God shall call. And with many other words did he testify and exhort, saying, Save yourselves from this untoward generation.

Then they that gladly received his word were baptized: and the same day there were added unto them about three thousand souls. And they continued stedfastly in the apostles' doctrine and fellowship, and in breaking of bread, and in prayers. And fear came upon every soul: and many wonders and signs were done by the apostles. And all that believed were together, and had all things common; And sold their possessions and goods, and parted them to all men, as every man had need. And they, continuing daily with one accord in the temple, and breaking bread from house to house, did eat their meat with gladness and singleness of heart, Praising God, and having favour with all the people. And the Lord added to the church daily such as should be saved.

REGIONAL REFORMATION

Often, we equate revival to a strong, consistent outpouring of God's presence where miracles, signs, and wonders, easily and constantly manifest. This is factual in thought; however, if a ministry is truly mantling revival fire, the revival should eventually impact the:

❖ Land
❖ Community
❖ Climate
❖ Atmosphere
❖ Economic Production
❖ Political Government
❖ Spiritual Enlightenment
❖ Family Lifestyle
❖ Generational Disposition & Inheritance

True revival is not void of reformation. We know true revival has come to a region when:

- Deliverance, healing, and wellness are evident in people, families, generations, the land, communities, atmospheres, and region.

- The sins and curses of the people and land are broken, producing the production, fruitfulness, fullness, multiplication, subduing, and dominion that God originally designed in *Genesis 1:28*.

- The blessings of *Deuteronomy 28* over takes the region as honor the commandments of God with their life.

- A renewal of belief and faith in God is restored into the region.

- The reestablishing of salvation is restored people, families, lands, climate, atmospheres, communities, and regions.

- Whole families serve God as his name and wonders are glorified throughout the generations.

- There is reconciliation and restoration of restored covenant with God where people walk in destiny relationship with him and live through his word, morals, standards, character, and nature.

- People live a lifestyle of prayer, fasting, studying the word, and building themselves up in the identity, destiny, and wellness of God.

- People cry out in repentance and are restored to salvation, just by the presence of God reigning in the region.

- People are added to God's kingdom daily as the fame of regional revival spreads like wild fire, drawing souls within the region and beyond, to be saved and live for Jesus.

- The gifts of the spirit stir and tangibly manifest in the saints and ministries.

- People are consistently equipped, licensed, ordained, and released to walk in their destiny and calling.

- Improvements and amendments of what is wrong, corrupt, unsatisfactory, evil, abusive, out of order, is reordered in the will and purpose of God and his kingdom.

- Change for the betterment of the people, families, lands, climates, atmospheres, and communities is tangible and evident.

- Principalities, powers, and territorial spirits are displaced from the region, and God's Holy principalities - his fivefold ministers - govern and guard the gates of the region.

- High places and hidden covens are torn down, as idols are exposed and dismantled, and witches and warlocks are given an ultimatum to serve God or be judged to damnation.

- The climate and atmospheres of homes, communities and eventually the entire region begins to radiate the goodness, blessing, and glory of God as the region lives under an open heaven where God's covering, protection, government, and kingdom is established and reigns.

- God's government overrides the Worldly system as the political arenas within the community seek Godly counsel and guidance for what laws, standards, and practices should be allowed in the region.

- People seek God and ministries before they consider worldly systems of wellness and success.

- Poverty and lack are SHIFTED out as sufficient employment, entrepreneurship, opportunities for personal and community advancement, is SHIFTED into the region.

- Rebuilding of the physical face of the communities where walls, businesses, homes, organizations, churches, and the land itself begins to manifest the glory, beauty, wealth, and wellness of God.

- Godly people and ministries become land owners and begin to take back the region for the kingdom of God.

- Godly people and ministries build their own schools and universities to professionally educate and equip the saints in their destiny and calling.

- Godly people and ministries build their own houses, hospitals, wellness centers, banks, stores, malls, counseling centers, gyms, social service agencies, schools, shelters, social ventures; the world pursues the Godly to get their needs and desires met.

Conclusion: We must desire more than a great move of God inside the walls of our church and events. Our mindsets and focus must be to take over the region with the glory and kingdom of God.

THE IDENTITY OF A REVIVALIST

It is essential that revivalist know who they are. Identity is vital to operating in the strength, armor, splendor, protection, dominion, and authority of the Lord. God has literally dressed the revivalist to make sure they are equipped to carry the mantle of revival fire. We discern this through the life of Aaron and the design of the priestly garments in *Exodus 28*.

Aaron's name means *"light bringer."* He was the priestly revivalist of the Israelites in his day. His very life, even his garments were significant to his identity and calling as a revivalist. How he presented himself to the people and to God was significant in him being able to adequately fulfill his duties. God required special garments because he wanted him to be distinguished with dominion glory and beauty.

> *Exodus 28:2-4 And thou shalt make holy garments for Aaron thy brother for glory and for beauty. And thou shalt speak unto all that are wise hearted, whom I have filled with the spirit of wisdom, that they may make Aaron's garments to consecrate him, that he may minister unto me in the priest's office.*

Glory is *"Kabod"* in the Hebrew and is indicative of the *"weight, reputation, honor, splendor, reverence and dignity"* of Aaron's call as a revivalist. It was not to be taken lightly, as the literal revival glory fire of God was upon his shoulders.

Beauty is *"tipara"* in the Hebrew and is representative of the *"bravery, honor, excellence, stature, rank, favor, and glamor"* he carried as a revivalist. Beauty was also an indicator of how pleasing and attractive the light that Aaron carried was appealing to God. God wanted to be wooed and drawn to Aaron as he offered atonement on behalf of the people in the most holy place, so he required attractive, specific, expensive garments for that purpose.

Aaron's garments could not be made by just anyone, as not everyone could comprehend and create the dominion glory and beauty that signified his identity and calling. God told Moses to gather the wise hearted, those full the spirit of wisdom who could consecrate Aaron, such that he could minister in his priestly office as a revivalist.

Wisdom is _hakema_ in the Hebrew and means:
1. skillful, wisely, wit, wise
2. skill (in war)
3. wisdom (in administration)
4. shrewdness, prudence (in religious affairs)
5. wisdom (ethical and religious)

The wise men had a heart, intellect, and revelation of who Aaron was to God and to Israel. They were able to war for it and possessed the skills and shrewdness to armor and consecrate him for God's glory. Everyone will not be able to be in your inner circle, cultivate you, empower you, or carry you in the spirit as a revivalist. It will take wise people who understand the dominion glory and beauty on your life, can honor you and your calling, and are committed to making sure you are consecrated in the office God has granted to your hands.

The consecrating represented a setting apart to fulfill the work of the Lord. Consecration encompasses purity, holiness, sanctity, dedication, sacrifice, separation and distinction from the common.

- ✓ Revivalists cannot and will not be able to do or get away with what others may seem to.
- ✓ They will not be able to go where everyone else goes.
- ✓ The revival fire that they carry cannot be exposed to just anyone.

Even though others will glean from it, the revival fire is intertwined in the revivalist's very identity and is set apart for God. This is the reason Aaron making the golden calf was so detrimental (**Study Exodus 32-34**).

> **Exodus 32:1-4** *When the people saw that Moses was so long in coming down from the mountain, they gathered around Aaron and said, "Come, make us gods who will go before us. As for this fellow Moses who brought us up out of Egypt, we don't know what has happened to him." Aaron answered them, "Take off the gold earrings that your wives, your sons and your daughters are wearing, and bring them to me." So all the people took off their earrings and brought them to Aaron. He took what they handed him and made it into an idol cast in the shape of a calf, fashioning it with a tool. Then they said, "These are your gods, Israel, who brought you up out of Egypt."*

Though Aaron knew God, knew how to seek God, knew his laws and standards, and knew he was a jealous God, he built and offered the people a counterfeit. He took his revival fire that was only to be offered to the Lord and created an idol god. He then created an altar before it, proclaimed a feast, and prepared himself and the people to sacrifice unto a god he fashioned through his revival fire.

> **Verse 5-6** *And when Aaron saw it, he built an altar before it; and Aaron made proclamation, and said, Tomorrow is a feast to the Lord. And they rose up early on the morrow, and offered burnt offerings, and brought peace offerings;*

and the people sat down to eat and to drink, and rose up to play.

Aaron was out of order. He became common. He allowed the people to dictate to him as a high priest, rather than remaining grounded in the standards that God had set for his life and for the people. He also allowed the people to breach his counsel of only being directed and cultivated by God and the wise hearted who understood his calling. Aaron therefore, defiled his identity and calling, his office as a high priest, and his revival light that made him attractive and distinguished unto the Lord. Had he remained set apart, and not lend his ear to people who did not honor the glory and beauty upon his life, he would not have succumb to making the golden calf.

As a revivalist, you must live inside the holy place and remain amongst those who can value and protect the call upon your life. Those who know your importance and will do nothing to tempt you to sacrifice it. The minute you come out of this place, you will yield to please the people rather than honor God. You resort to making the revival fire blaze how the people want it to be rather than what God requires it to be. Or you fashion the revival fire through the abilities, gifts, and talents that come with your mantle rather than through the will, intent, and purpose of God. And because you are a representative of revival fire, your very identity is sacrificed along with whatever you fashion for the people.

At Aaron, the revivalist's leading, the Israelites became their own corruption. There was even a war sound radiating from the camp where their actions caused a war among them even though no one was attacking them. Their own sin and idolatry became enmity unto them.

Exodus 32:7-8 And the Lord said unto Moses, Go, get thee down; for thy people, which thou broughtest out of the land of Egypt, have corrupted themselves: They have turned aside quickly out of the way which I commanded them: they have made them a molten calf, and have worshipped it, and have sacrificed thereunto, and said, These be thy gods, O Israel, which have brought thee up out of the land of Egypt.

Exodus 32:17-18 And when Joshua heard the noise of the people as they shouted, he said unto Moses, There is a noise of war in the camp. And he said, It is not the voice of them that shout for mastery, neither is it the voice of them that cry for being overcome: but the noise of them that sing do I hear.

It was not a sound that provoked or proclaimed the Lord Jesus Christ. It was not a sound of fighting victoriously against enemies. It was not even a sound of being sieged by the enemy. It was a sound of defilement in the camp of the Israelites. This sound ignited the wrath and revival judgment of God.

Exodus 32:27-28 And he said unto them, Thus saith the Lord God of Israel, Put every man his sword by his side, and go in and out from gate to gate throughout the camp, and slay every man his brother, and every man his companion, and every man his neighbour. And the children of Levi did according to the word of Moses: and there fell of the people that day about three thousand men.

Exodus 32:35 And the Lord plagued the people, because they made the calf, which Aaron made.

Even with repentance and consecration, there are extreme consequences when a revivalist operates contrary to the Lord. Because we live in God's presence, he expects us to demonstrate his character, nature, and identity regardless of what others choose to do. He expects us to have reverential fear for his holiness that is around and in us, and to never defile his revival fire that we carry. This is because everything about their calling and identity has purpose and is a dedication unto the Lord. Lets' look at Aaron's revival garment in more detail.

Figure 1http://narrowgateentrance.com/priest-garments/

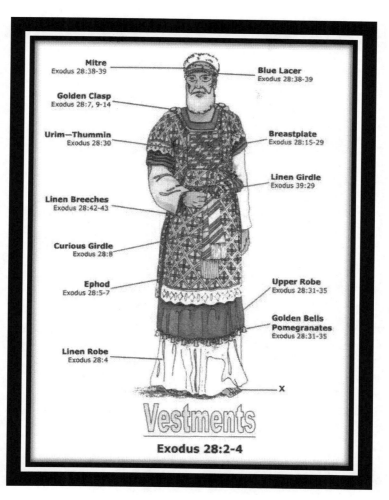

Figure 2Figure 2 http://www.british-israel.us/185.html

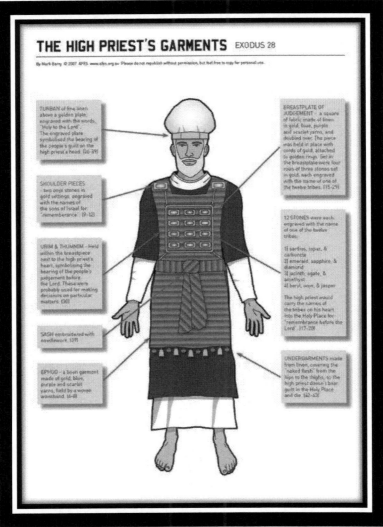

Figure 3Figure 2 http://www.british-israel.us/185.html

High priests embody the sins and blessings of the:

> ➤ People
> ➤ Generations - past, present, and future
> ➤ Regions and spheres of influence that are promised to the people
> ➤ Chosen tribes amongst the people

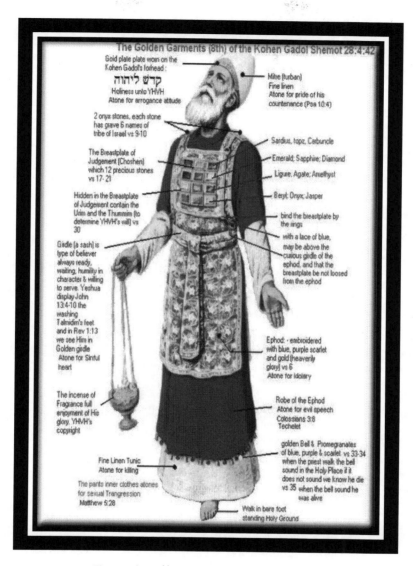

The Golden Garments (8th) of the Kohen Gadol Shemot 28:4:42

Gold plate plate worn on the Kohen Gadol's forhead :

קֹדֶשׁ לַיהוה

Holiness unto YHVH
Atone for arrogance attitude

Mitre (turban)
Fine linen
Atone for pride of his countenance (Psa 10:4)

2 onyx stones, each stone has grave 6 names of tribe of Israel vs 9-10

The Breastplate of Judgement (Choshen) which 12 precious stones vs 17- 21

Hidden in the Breastplate of Judgement contain the Urim and the Thummim (to determine YHVH's will) vs 30

Sardius, topz, Carbuncle

Emerald; Sapphire; Diamond

Ligure, Agate; Amethyst

Beryl; Onyx; Jasper

bind the breastplate by the rings

Girdle (a sash) is type of believer always ready, waiting, humility in character & willing to serve. Yeshua display John 13:4-10 the washing Talmidim's feet and in Rev 1:13 we see Him in Golden girdle Atone for Sinful heart

with a lace of blue, may be above the curious girdle of the ephod, and that the breastplate be not loosed from the ephod

The incense of Fragrance full enjoyment of His glory. YHVH's copyright

Ephod: - embroidered with blue, purple scarlet and gold (heavenly glory) vs 6
Atone for idolary

Robe of the Ephod
Atone for evil speech
Colossians 3:8
Techelet

golden Bell & Promegranates of blue, purple & scarlet vs 33-34 when the priest walk the bell sound in the Holy Place if it does not sound we know he die vs 35 when the bell sound he was alive

Fine Linen Tunic
Atone for killing

The pants inner clothes atones for sexual Trangression Matthew 5:28

Walk in bare foot standing Holy Ground

Figure 4 http://www.british-israel.us/185.html

High priests embody the:

- ➢ Headship government of God and his kingdom
- ➢ Holiness of God
- ➢ Righteous heart of God

- Unadulterated truth of God
- Weighty Kabod glory of God
- Judgment of God against sin and defilement
- Fire of God to refine what is of him and sacrifice that which is not of him
- Fragrance of God to offer up sweetness unto God, while filling the atmosphere with his aroma
- Sound of God that gives access to his countenance
- Adornment of God to display his beauty, honor, and splendor
- Linen of God that portrays his modesty, purity, and enablement to sacrifice unto God for the atonement of sins
- Humility, servitude, heart, posture, and submission of the people, land, and region unto God as a lifestyle of covenant with him

The high priest is armored in the essence of God, which is their identity. They are not just a unique representation of him, they embody the essence of him. Though Jesus came as the great high priest and became the ultimate sacrifice for our sins, revivalists continue to serve as high priest who carry the essence of God in the earth, to provoke people to boldly walk in the eternal salvation that Jesus restored to all mankind.

> *Hebrews 4:16-17 Seeing then that we have a great high priest, that is passed into the heavens, Jesus the Son of God, let us hold fast our profession. For we have not an high priest which cannot be touched with the feeling of our infirmities; but was in all points tempted like as we are, yet without sin. Let us therefore come boldly unto the throne of*

grace that we may obtain mercy, and find grace to help in time of need.

Revivalist are no longer the sacrifice to kill death; they are the sacrifice to awaken eternal life. The mantle is the same, but the posture and disposition has changed. Revivalist must be examples of God that lead people into the mercy and grace of Jesus, so they can live the eternal life Jesus provided for them. Be cognizant of the revival mantle you carry, and know that you can never sacrifice, make common, or take lightly, the revival fire that blazes from your identity. **SHIFT!**

HOLY GHOST & FIRE

Many want revival, but they:
- ✓ Do not want the Holy Spirit
- ✓ Only want a measure of the Holy Spirit
- ✓ Only want the part of the Holy Spirit that they understand
- ✓ Want to control the Holy Spirit

Revival is not contained by man, but by the Spirit of God. You cannot have revival without the fullness of the Holy Spirit at work. You cannot build revival upon a man or a ministry. If it is not built upon the fullness of the Holy Spirit, it will die.

> *2Corinthians 3:17 Now the Lord is that Spirit: and where the Spirit of the Lord is, there is liberty.*

The Holy Spirit must have free reign and immeasurable liberty. Otherwise, you just have a good event or movement, but you are not experiencing true revival.

True revival takes surrendering to the Holy Spirit which starts through relationship with God and his presence. It also requires an understanding of the purpose of the Holy Spirit.

> *Luke 24:49 And, behold, I send the promise of my Father upon you: but tarry ye in the city of Jerusalem, until ye be endued with power from on high.*

> *John 14:16-17 And I will pray the Father, and he shall give you another Comforter, that he may abide with you for ever; Even the Spirit of truth; whom the world cannot receive, because it seeth him not, neither knoweth him: but ye know him; for he dwelleth with you, and shall be in you.*

John 14:26 But the Advocate, the Holy Spirit, whom the Father will send in my name, will teach you all things and will remind you of everything I have said to you.

John 15:26 But when the Comforter is come, whom I will send unto you from the Father, even the Spirit of truth, who proceeds from the Father, he shall testify of me.

John 16:13 Howbeit when he, the Spirit of truth, is come, he will guide you into all truth: for he shall not speak of himself; but whatsoever he shall hear, that shall he speak: and he will shew you things to come.

The Holy Spirit was sent to:

Dwell with us Romans 8:9	Be among us John 14:16-17	Guide us John 16:13	Endues us with power Luke 24:49
Live inside us Luke 24:49	Teach us John 14:26	Comfort us John 15:26	Liberate us 2Corinthians 3:17
Reveal Godly truth John 16:13	Sanctifies us 2Thessalonians 2:13	Regenerates us John 3:5-8	Empowers us Luke 4:14
Fills us Ephesians 5:18	Reveals Christ to us John 16:14-15	Bears witness in us Romans 8:16	Anoints us Luke 4:18
Renews us Titus 3:5	Unifies us Ephesians 4:3	Instill spiritual fruit Galatians 5:22-23	Distributes gifts 1Corinthians 12:4
Secures & seals us 2Corinthians 1:22	Seal of redemption Ephesians 1:13	Frees us Romans 8:2	Speaks/Through us 1Corinthians 12:3
Quickens our bodies	Transforms us	Instill patience Galatians 5:5	Grants eternal life Galatians 6:8

Romans 8:11	2Corinthians 3:18		
Supplies us Philippians 1:19	**Corporate indwelling** Ephesians 2:22	**Strengths us** Ephesians 3:16	**Reveal mysteries** Ephesians 3:5
Cast out demons Matthew 12:28	**Loves through us** Romans 5:5	**Moves & Shifts us** 2Peter 1:21	**Preaches through us** 1Peter 1:12
Testifies of Jesus 1John 3:24	**Instills obedience** 1John 3:24	**Infuses Joy** 1Thessalonians 1:6	**Does kingdom works** Acts 20:28
Baptizes us with fire Matthew 3:11-12	**Judges Ungodliness** Matthew 3:11-12	**Makes Intercession** Ephesians 6:19	**Creates** Genesis 1:1-2

God makes it clear that we need the Holy Spirit. He intends for his Holy Spirit to be the ultimate director and strength of our lives and all that he sets our hands to do. God himself operated through the Holy Spirit to create the earth.

> *Genesis 1:1-2 In the beginning God created the heaven and the earth. And the earth was without form, and void; and darkness was upon the face of the deep. And the Spirit of God moved upon the face of the waters.*

The Holy Spirit is a master creator, planter, plower, builder, establisher, and sustainer of God's kingdom. There is no revival without the Holy Spirit.

> *Matthew 3:11-12 I indeed baptize you with water unto repentance: but he that cometh after me is mightier than I, whose shoes I am not worthy to bear: he shall baptize you with the Holy Ghost, and with fire: Whose fan is in his hand, and he*

*will thoughly purge his floor, and gather his wheat into the
garner; but he will burn up the chaff with unquenchable fire.*

The Holy Spirit baptizes us, our land, and region in his
presence and with revival fire. As we are baptized, the
essence of who we and our sphere, is thoroughly purged
and cleansed. That which presents as Godly and beneficial –
the wheat – is stored inside his presence, while that which is
considered *chaff* is burned with unquenchable fire.

Dictionary.com defines *chaff* as:
1. the husks of grains and grasses that are separated during
   threshing
2. straw cut up for fodder
3. worthless matter
4. synonyms: garbage, dross, rubbish, trash
5. informal junk, schlock; vulgar "slang crap"

Chaff is that which is ungodly, unhealthy, or unnecessary for
our lives, destiny, ministries, business, land, communities,
atmospheres, climates, regions, and nations. An
unquenchable fire is an eternal judging fire. The Strong's
concordance defines it as an *"an eternal hell fire to punish the
damned."* As the Holy Spirit baptizes us and revives us with
resurrection life, it judges the unholy within us, while
tormenting and destroying it with an eternal fire.

So basically, when the Holy Spirit comes into our lives, he
- Baptizes us with his presence
- Baptizes us with revival fire
- Destroys sin and evil with a judging fire.

He has two fires, each eternal, but completing different tasks
to make sure we look like, act like, and represent God and
his kingdom.

37

When we quench the Holy Spirit, we quench his FIRES. When the Holy Spirit is not allowed to be free in our lives and regions, he cannot actively fulfill his working where the fullness of salvation manifests. We love his presence and want his revival fire, yet we must position ourselves to let him burn up the chaff in our lives. That includes letting him burn up our fears, our unbelief, our lack or wavering faith, our religion, our insecurities, our vulnerabilities, our lack of understanding and misunderstanding concerning him, and our need to control him. When we do not give him free reign, this chaff works against his presence and FIRES in our lives. What should be eternally destroyed is being exposed through our thoughts and behaviors, because it has not been properly disposed of through the workings of the Holy Spirit.

Baptism means to immerse, purify, and to totally submerge. When we are baptized by fire, we are totally submerged. If we are controlling or only allowing a measure of the Holy Spirit to operate in our lives and spheres of influence, then we should examine ourselves as to whether we have been baptized by fire.

> ➤ Maybe you are baptized in his presence, but not baptized in his presence AND fire.
> ➤ Maybe you have received the gift of the Holy Spirit, and he has come upon or lives in you, but his fullness has not been allowed to operate yet.

Revival will not be fully impactful or long lasting with measure. When the Holy Spirit is not fully operational, we resort to setting rules and standards within the revival awakening in an effort to control what we do not understand. The Holy Spirit is a comforter, so he does not impose himself upon us. He respects our boundaries and right to choose what of God we desire, yet this quenches his presence, revival fire, and unquenchable fire. I want to give you a few strategies for developing a friendship with the Holy Spirit, so you can trust him with helping you to ignite revival in your life, region, and sphere of influence.

Receiving Holy Spirit as Friend

We are always longing for someone else to comfort us, guide us, teach us, empower us, intercede for us, advocate for us, etc. Though there is nothing wrong with desiring relationships and support, the Holy Spirit should be our best friend and should be the example of how we are to engage and govern every other relationship in our lives.

Jesus said that though the world would not be able to receive the Holy Spirit, we should be able to know and recognize him, for he lives with us constantly and will be in us. That the world does not know what he looks like or what to look for, but we should know because he will be staying with us and will live in us.

> *John 14-16-17 The Amplified Bible And I will ask the Father, and He will give you another Comforter (Counselor, Helper, Intercessor, Advocate, Strengthener, and Standby), that He may remain with you forever — The Spirit of Truth, Whom the world cannot receive (welcome, take to its heart), because it does not see him or know and recognize him. But you know and recognize him, for He lives with you [constantly] and will be in you.*

See is Theoreo in the Greek and means:

1. to be a spectator of, to discern, intensively (acknowledge) behold, consider, look on, perceive
2. to be a spectator, look at, behold, to view attentively, take a view of
3. survey, to view mentally, consider, to see, to perceive with the eyes, to enjoy the presence of one

4. to discern, descry to ascertain, find out by seeing

Know is *Ginosko* in the Greek and means:
1. allow, be aware (of), feel, (have) know (- ledge), perceived, be resolved, can speak, be sure, understand
2. to learn, to know, come to know, get a knowledge of, perceive, feel to become known
3. to understand, to know, Jewish idiom for sexual intercourse between a man and a woman, to become acquainted with

The world cannot discern the Holy Spirit, but we should be able to. We should be able to know him and become acquainted with him as we would our spouse or someone we love. We acknowledge the Holy Spirit when we want his presence or the attributes of his character, such as his healing power or blessing; however, we do not intensively behold him in relationship as a loved one, as we would a spouse or friend. Though we are the ones who are to know him, the Holy Spirit is constantly spurned and ostracized because of his position in our lives. Every time we dreadfully or lustfully wish for someone else or something else without initially drawing into the Holy Spirit, we reject, grieve and ostracized the Holy Spirit. For it is as if the one gift Jesus left to comfort us and be with us forever, we reject over and over and over and over again.

> **Verse 18** *I will not leave you comfortless: I will come to you.*

Jesus obviously knew there would be lonely days. Days where others would forsake us; days where we would feel exposed, misunderstood, rejected, betrayed, uncertain, grieved, etc. Days where our spouses and friends would not be sufficient comfort for us. Days where only relationship with him would fulfill us. Days where we would need

Godly truth and to be guided into the knowledge of divine truth.

- ❖ I would encourage you to study the scriptures regarding the Holy Spirit and begin to spend time with the Holy Spirit like never before.
- ❖ Ask him to teach you his thoughts and ways and to cultivate a relationship with you where he becomes your best friend and first choice for comfort, guidance, support, empowerment, etc.
- ❖ Ask the Holy Spirit his likes and dislikes, and repent quickly when you grieve the Holy Spirit (*Study Ephesians 4:30, Matthew 12:31-32), Hebrews 10:26-29, Acts 5:3, Acts 7:51*)
- ❖ Ask the Holy Spirit to teach you how to consistently implement what he says, such that God's will and purpose becomes your lifestyle.
- ❖ Do not move on a matter without the voice of the Holy Spirit. Get his counsel and direction before making decisions.
- ❖ Include the Holy Spirit when you are praying and studying your word. Ask him what and who he wants you to pray for, how you should spend your prayer time (soak, warfare, intercession, decreeing, etc.). Ask him what you should study and to give you revelation of what you are studying.
- ❖ Ask him to help you discern between truth and deceit, especially when you are in seasons of warfare, stressed, weary, experiencing a challenging situation, are overly emotional, feeling lonely or ostracized, etc.
- ❖ When you find yourself obsessed or drawn more to a person or thing, repent quickly and reconnect to the Holy Spirit.
- ❖ When you start to feel lonely, depressed, overly emotional, immediately seek comfort and love from the Holy Spirit.

- ❖ Ask Holy Spirit to baptize you in his presence and two fires.
- ❖ Ask him to kill any vulnerabilities, religion, need to control, unbelief, lack of understanding, misunderstanding about him, and to give you clear revelation and an impartation of his character, his nature, and his role in your life.

Holy Spirit Operations
- ❖ As you commit to evolving into the character and nature of the Holy Spirit, ask him to give you clarity about how he operates. Ask him to teach you to discern and operate in his gifts, character, and fruit; and to provide opportunities for you to grow and mature in each area.

  - ➤ Gifts of the Spirit (*Study 1Corinthians 12, Isaiah 11:2-3, Ephesians 4:11--16*)
  - ➤ Character of the Holy Spirit (*Study John 3:1-5, 1Corinthians 12, Ephesians 1:13–14; 5:18*)
  - ➤ Fruit of the spirit (*Study Galatians 5:22-23*)

- ❖ Ask the Holy Spirit how he manifests in people, services, and regions, and to teach you to discern when it is him or strange fire, as some things tend to be equated to the Holy Spirit, but are not the Holy Spirit. But that can only be discerned by his Spirit as the Holy Spirit can operate and manifest in unusual and peculiar ways, or our flesh can respond to the Holy Spirit in unusual and peculiar ways.

- ❖ Since you will be operating in team and regional ministry, as you ignite revival, ask Holy Spirit to teach you how different ethnic groups and cultures respond to the Holy Spirit. I heard a great apostolic revivalist by the name of Ryan Lestrange, share revelation of how African Americans tend to shout, speak in loud tongues, and bind devils when the strong presence of the Holy Spirit manifest. Yet Caucasians tend to get quiet while soaking, laughing, jerking, and enjoying the presence of the Lord. He shared that neither is wrong as it is a difference in culture. Yet there can be much judgment between the two groups when they are worshipping together, due to the lack of respect for culture and ethnicity. I agree with this revelation and have witnessed other cultures who laugh uncontrollable, roll on the floor, and display extreme jerking motions when a strong presence of the Holy Spirit manifests. I had to ask the Holy Spirit if it was it him and he explained to me that it was. It is easy to just judge without asking him and go to binding demons and calling good evil, and evil good. Practice discerning by and through the Holy Spirit.

Walking By The Spirit Versus Flesh

❖ Ask the Holy Spirit to teach you how to have Spirit to Spirit encounters with him where you are not just experiencing his presence, but are truly being empowered, enlightened, rejuvenated, and transformed by his presence, his voice, and your relationship with him. As the Holy Spirit is teaching you Spirit to Spirit encounters:

> ➢ Be obedient to what the Holy Spirit speaks.

> ➢ Stay in the process of deliverance, healing, and maturation until the Holy Spirit gives you further direction. Do not abort the process by giving into emotions, frustration, or implementing your own plans.

> ➢ Do not expect the Holy Spirit to always perform for you. If he does not speak or you do not hear him, do not assume that he is not there or that he

is not working. Though God is touched by feelings, he is not a feeling. We are not going to always feel him. God is sovereign; he operates by the truth and Spirit of who he is. We should know he is with us and that he is active in the relationship with us, even when he is silent, and even when our flesh and emotions are not feeling his tangible presence.

God is touched by our feelings, so we can boldly approach him and know that he is willing to help us regardless to whether he says or does anything.

Hebrews 4:14-16 Seeing then that we have a great high priest, that is passed into the heavens, Jesus the Son of God, let us hold fast our profession. For we have not an high priest which cannot be touched with the feeling of our infirmities; but was in all points tempted like as we are, yet without sin. Let us therefore come boldly unto the throne of grace that we may obtain mercy, and find grace to help in time of need.
Learn to walk in the Spirit and not by emotions and flesh.

Galatians 5:16-25 This I say then, Walk in the Spirit, and ye shall not fulfill the lust of the flesh. For the flesh lusteth against the Spirit, and the Spirit against the flesh: and these are contrary the one to the other: so that ye cannot do the things that ye would…..(Study the rest of this passage of scripture).

Spirit to Spirit worship, worships God for who he is and what his word says and not according to feeling, or what God is doing or not doing. This level of worship is sovereign as God is sovereign. It is being in relationship with God simply

44

because he is God and because of the truth of his word. So even when we do not feel him, hear him, or when he is not moving how we desire, we remain in connection with him through the knowledge that he is always with us, he has a plan for us, and his plans and word for us is yes and Amen. They will not return void, and they will come to pass as we grow and advance in our walk with him.

John 4:23-24 *But the hour cometh, and now is, when the true worshippers shall worship the Father in spirit and in truth: for the Father seeketh such to worship him. God is a Spirit: and they that worship him must worship him in spirit and in truth.*

The Message Version *It's who you are and the way you live that count before God. Your worship must engage your spirit in the pursuit of truth. That's the kind of people the Father is out looking for: those who are simply and honestly themselves before him in their worship. God is sheer being itself — Spirit. Those who worship him must do it out of their very being, their spirits, their true selves, in adoration.*

When we hang out with our friends, sometimes we do nothing. We just sit in a room and are with one another. As we pursue relationship with the Holy Spirit, we should do the same thing, while trusting that even when nothing is going on, we are building relationship by spending time, and God is right there in the midst of us. He is spending time just being with us.

Deuteronomy 31:8 *It is the Lord who goes before you. he will be with you; he will not leave you or forsake you. Do not fear or be dismayed."*

45

Deuteronomy 31:6 Be strong and courageous. Do not fear or be in dread of them, for it is the Lord your God who goes with you. he will not leave you or forsake you

Psalm 73:23-26 Nevertheless, I am continually with you; you hold my right hand. You guide me with your counsel, and afterward you will receive me to glory. Whom have I in heaven but you? And there is nothing on earth that I desire besides you. My flesh and my heart may fail, but God is the strength of my heart and my portion forever.

Zephaniah 3:17 The Amplified Bible The Lord your God is in the midst of you, a Mighty One, a Savior [Who saves]! he will rejoice over you with joy; he will rest [in silent satisfaction] and in his love he will be silent and make no mention [of past sins, or even recall them]; he will exult over you with singing.

Reject Complacency

❖ Never become complacent in your relationship with the Holy Spirit. Always seek to go deeper and higher in learning and growing in him. If you find yourself becoming complacent or stagnant, search out what may be blocking you from SHIFTING deeper. Blockages could be fear, insecurity, not feeling in control, a curse or stronghold, unforgiveness, release, etc. Control is a big hindrance to going deeper. To sufficiently mature in God and reach destiny, it is necessary to surrender in trusting and totally being vulnerable in him. Spend time commanding your Spirit to go higher and deeper in your relationship with the Holy Spirit.

➢ Repent for any areas you have not relinquished control or have not submitted your will to God.

➤ Repent for fears of giving up control and release forgiveness to anyone that you have given control of your life, but they have misused or taken advantage of your trust.

➤ Build your trust in God by decreeing out scriptures in the areas of trust, faith, and belief if necessary, as this will further cleanse any blockages, walls, and lingering strongholds in this area. I usually cleanse by soaking in the blood of Jesus. I release the blood to cleanse all the effects of strongholds while commanding any spirits behind it to go. I then spend time soaking in the healing glory of God.

➤ Study scriptures on going higher and deeper in God, and on healing. Meditate on them as you are commanding your spirit to go higher and deeper.

➤ Ask the Holy Spirit what the next phase of intimacy with him is, and to give you tools to work on to cultivate and accelerate into that next level of relationship.

Speaking In Tongues

❖ If you do not speak in your prayer language, ask the Holy Spirit to give you your prayer language. Spend time daily building yourself up by speaking in tongues.

➤ Speaking in tongues is a gift. You do not have to work by tarrying for it. If you study tarrying, it is simply waiting on the Holy Spirit to empower you, and if you have been pursuing the Holy Spirit as your friend, then you are already spending time waiting and resting in his presence.

➤ Speaking in tongues truly is a faith act of opening your mouth and speaking as the Holy Spirit leads. Through our prayer language comes an increased power and guidance of the Holy Spirit to speak the voice of God, operate in giftings and live a life of holiness. Without the evidence of tongues, one is basically living the actions of the intimacy and comfort of the Holy Spirit without the actual intimacy and love language of having the Holy Spirit indwelling in their lives. One thing we will learn from our relationship with the Holy Spirit is that intimacy is power. It is motivating, refreshing, reviving, strengthening, and accelerating (just think about how you feel when you are with someone you love). Though one may have the Holy Spirit, without the evidence of speaking in tongues, one is limited in their ability to express their feelings to God and for God to express himself through them, as the Holy Spirit makes intercession for us through groanings that we cannot express or explain through our earthly comprehension or our earthly expressions.

Romans 8:26 Likewise the Spirit also helpeth our infirmities: for we know not what we should pray for as we ought: but the Spirit itself maketh intercession for us with groanings which cannot be uttered.

Also without speaking in tongues, one is limited only to their native or learned language which is truly a soulish experience. But tongues liberate a person from the soulish to the spirit realm, where they can be empowered to experience God and his mysteries on levels that the soul cannot go. This is not about the soul being carnal. When we operate in our soul, we tend to operate in our mind, will, and intellect, so we

48

tend to limit things by what we know, what feels good, or what feels comfortable. However, when we operate in God from Spirit to Spirit, we are more apt to be submissive to the unknowing. All our earthly boundaries are removed, and we are inside a realm of unlimited potential - where his spirit is guiding and controlling our experience in God rather than us being in control.

Speaking in tongues elevates a believer to a place in God where God can reveal mysteries to us. These mysteries cannot be revealed and sometimes even understood, by those who do not have the evidence of speaking in tongues.

1Corinthians 14:2 *For he that speaketh in an unknown tongue speaketh not unto men, but unto God: for no man understandeth him; howbeit in the spirit he speaketh mysteries.*

The Message Version *If you praise him in the private language of tongues, God understands you but no one else does, for you are sharing intimacies just between you and him.*

Hindrances to not immediately speaking in tongues:
- ❖ Fear of the manifestation of tongues itself.
- ❖ Fearing the mysteries of the process of speaking in tongues.
- ❖ Fear of being vulnerable (losing control) and submitting to the presence of God and giving up their need to be in control or fear of being vulnerable before others.
- ❖ Fear of how they will sound or what others will say.

49

❖ Fear of the intimacy of tongues because one has to surrender and be intimate with God in order to yield themselves to the experience of the Holy Spirit. The 120 people in *Acts 2* was lingering; they were just waiting around for God. They deemed him worth the wait. Many do not know how to be intimate, therefore, they fail to tap into a place of receiving.

❖ Tradition and religious beliefs.

❖ Ignorance or lack of knowledge and understanding.

❖ Not feeling worthy of God's gift.

❖ Sin blockage or shame, guilt, and condemnation still being present, due to past or present sin in one's life.

❖ Demonic strongholds can hinder the infilling of the Holy Spirit.

❖ Fortune Telling, Satanism, Witchcraft, Horoscopes, Ouija Boards, Spiritism, or other non-Christian religions practices that need to be renounced. You see, the occult involvement in our lives is not innocent child's play. It gives Satan legal access to our lives. (*Deuteronomy 18:10-12*). If a person is now going to seek supernatural guidance from God by his Holy Spirit, then they need to silence and break the powers of all other occult influences in Jesus' Name (*Acts 19:19*). They may even need to destroy all objects in their home or life that have supernatural ties. God speaks through our hearts, not through mediums or objects.

❖ The atmosphere may not be conducive to being able to receive. You, however, can create an atmosphere by praising and worshiping or declaring the scriptures.

❖ It may not be your time to receive an infilling. The Holy Spirit may want to build up anticipation, faith, and or relationship before manifesting the evidence of tongues.

Ask the Holy Spirit to help you to discern the reason you are not receiving your gift of tongues. Keep building a relationship with him, while asking him to give you your prayer language. He will not leave you desiring.

Luke 11:13 If you then, who are evil, know how to give good gifts to your children, how much more will the heavenly Father give the Holy Spirit to those who ask him!

Ephesians 5:18-21 And do not get drunk with wine, for that is debauchery, but be filled with the Spirit, addressing one another in psalms and hymns and spiritual songs, singing and making melody to the Lord with your heart, giving thanks always and for everything to God the Father in the name of our Lord Jesus Christ, submitting to one another out of reverence for Christ.

Psalms 84:11 For the LORD God is a sun and shield: the LORD will give grace and glory: no good thing will he withhold from them that walk uprightly

2Corinthians 1:20 For all the promises of God in him are yea, and in him Amen, unto the glory of God by us.

Decreeing limitless fruit, progression, and manifested glory, as you cultivate a relationship with the Holy Spirit. And as you are baptized in his presence, revival fire, and unquenchable fire. SHIFT!

BUILDING WORSHIPPERS

As we ignite revival, we cannot allow culture, ethnicity, personal or ministry beliefs, control issues, fears, insecurities, pride, mockery, witchcraft, new age expressions, or idolatry, rule our worship. Regardless of our differences, worship must be administered through the liberation of the Holy Spirit.

> **2Corinthians 3:17** *Now the Lord is that Spirit: and where the Spirit of the Lord is, there is liberty.*

Liberty means *"unrestrained, expressive, unorthodoxed, uncontrolled, unrestricted, unconstrained."*

Because we have cultural, ethical, and personal differences and vulnerability issues, we cannot assume that people are worshipping from a liberated disposition. When Jesus conversed with the woman at the well, he taught her how to worship.

> **John 4:23-24** *But an hour is coming, and now is, when the true worshipers will worship the Father in spirit and truth; for such people the Father seeks to be His worshipers. God is a Spirit: and they that worship him must worship him in spirit and in truth.*

Spirit is the very breath and essence of God. *Truth* is the reality concerning the identity, character, nature, and purposes of God. Therefore, worship is not what we want to offer God, but what he requires and deserves from us as worshippers. If we consider the posture of liberated worship, we would recognize that:

Only God should be worshiped:

- ***Deuteronomy 5:7*** *You shall have no other gods before Me.*

- ***Psalm 96:4-5*** *For great is the LORD and greatly to be praised; He is to be feared above all gods. For all the gods of the peoples are idols, But the LORD made the heavens.*

Flesh cannot glory in God's presence: A lot of what we call worship is really flesh reacting to the presence of God. However, this is not true worship as the flesh will express itself in excitement, uneasiness, confusion, lack of control, being overwhelmed, fearful, or in terror to the presence of God. None of this should ever exalt itself above God or your heart posture and intent of giving him due worship.

> ***1Corinthians*** *1:30 That no flesh should glory (boast) in his presence.*

Worship should be boastful & abandoned:

> ***Psalms 34:2*** *My soul shall make her boast in the LORD: the humble shall hear thereof, and be glad.*

<u>Boast</u> is *halal* <u>in the Hebrew and means:</u>
1. to be clear (orig. of sound, but usually of color)
2. to shine; hence, to make a show, to boast, to be (clamorously) foolish; to rave
3. to celebrate; also to stultify -- (make) boast (self), celebrate, commend
4. (deal, make), fool(- ish, -ly), glory, give (light), be (make, feign self) mad (against)
5. give in marriage, (sing, be worthy of) praise, rage, renowned, shine

When we are truly worshipping God, it should be as if we are giving ourselves into marriage.

- In marriage, we know the partner cleaves to his mate where they are yoked together. In worship, we should be cleaving to God, where we become one with him (*Genesis 2:24, Matthew 15:5*).

- Total submission, surrendering, and love that yields holy sanctification is required in marriage. God is the covering and head of the marriage (*Ephesians 5:22-26*). This must be displayed in our worship.

- Respect, obedience, and honor are required in marriage (*1Peter 3*). We should be relinquishing these attributes through our praise and worship.

- Though we should be modest and woo our husband, the woman's focus should be on internal adornment rather than external adornment in marriage. It should be about making sure our heart is appropriately postured and presentable to the Lord. We should not be prideful and more invested in our outward appearance in worship. We should be surrendered and invested in yielding our heart and soul to a posture that is humbled before God (*1Peter 3:3-5, James 4:2, Isaiah 3, 1Samuel 16:7*). When our internal nature is beautified, we are even more beautiful on the outside.

- Marriages are God ordained, honored and conformed into the his likeness (*Hebrews 13:4, Romans 12:2*). We should be striving to make worship what God wants it to be, not what we want it to be.

- There must be a Godly knowing and revelation of how God loves the church so that this love can be displayed in marriage through the husband who is the head (*Ephesians 5:25-27*). Many people have offense against the church, dread attending church, and forsake fellowship and even the assembly of the church, but claim to be offering up true worship unto God. We should ask God to show us and instill in us, his love for the church. If we do not know and love the body of Christ and God's church as God loves it, then we cannot fully worship him in spirit and in truth, as we have not given ourselves into marriage unto him.

- Husbands must be above reproach, married to one woman, temperament and self-controlled (*1Timothy 3:2*). The more we worship, the more we should begin to take on the character, nature, and identity of God, where our worship is displayed through our everyday actions. This is imperative because worship is not just an experience, it is a lifestyle. This scripture reveals a lifestyle posture of integral worship.

- There is covenant in marriage (*Matthew 19:6*). We must also understand that there is covenant in worship (*Deuteronomy 8:18, Psalms 89-3-4, Psalms 105:8-11. Nehemiah 1:5*)

The word *boast* further reveals that we should be so abandoned that we literally act like a mad person in our worship unto God. Even if we act like a mad person in God's presence, all glory should go to him. Our worship would be shinning, exalting and declaring who God is. Nothing about us should be seen or take center stage of his glory.

Should not be strange fire or witchcraft:

Exodus 30:7-9 And Aaron shall burn thereon sweet incense every morning: when he dresseth the lamps, he shall burn incense upon it. And when Aaron lighteth the lamps at even, he shall burn incense upon it, a perpetual incense before the Lord throughout your generations. Ye shall offer no strange incense thereon, nor burnt sacrifice, nor meat offering; neither shall ye pour drink offering thereon.

The incense was a symbol of the prayers and intercession of the people going up to God as a sweet fragrance. God wanted His dwelling to be a place where people could approach Him and pray to Him. *"...for my house will be called a house of prayer for all nations"* (**Isaiah 56:7**).

- **Psalms 141:2** *also confirm this as it declares: May my prayer be set before you like incense; may the lifting up of my hands be like the evening sacrifice.*

- **Roman 8:34** *contends that,"Christ Jesus, who died — more than that, who was raised to life — is at the right hand of God and is also interceding for us."*

Strange is *zur* in the Hebrew and means:
1. to turn aside (especially for lodging); hence to be a foreigner, strange, profane
2. specifically (active participle) to commit adultery - - (come from) another (man, place), fanner, go away, estrange, strange, stranger

Dictionary.com defines *profane* as:
1. characterized by irreverence or contempt for God or sacred principles or things; irreligious
2. not devoted to holy or religious purposes unconsecrated; secular (opposed to sacred)
3. unholy; heathen; pagan; not initiated into religious rites

or mysteries, as persons
4. common or vulgar
5. to misuse (anything that should be held in reverence or respect); defile; debase; employ basely or unworthily
6. to treat (anything sacred) with irreverence or contempt; violate the sanctity of

Dictionary.com defines *fanner* as:
1. to move, stir, or agitate (the air) with or as if with a fan
2. to cause air to blow upon, as from a fan; cool or refresh with or as if with a fan
3. to stir to activity with or as if with a fan: to fan a flame; to fan emotions
4. (of a breeze, current of air, etc.) to blow upon, as if driven by a fan

This is interesting because whatever we offer unto God is released into the atmosphere. We agitate and stir the atmosphere with it. We agitate and stir God with it. If it is strange, we are contaminating the atmosphere. We could also be stirring God to anger.

We must realize that anytime we do anything strange in our worship, to God we are committing adultery, being profane, turning away from him, and have become a foreigner in his sight.

- Being in the sanctuary that we built for him does not make it holy
- Being in his presence does not make it holy
- Sacrificing it as an offering does not make it holy
- Being chosen as a priest or glory carrier does not make it holy
- Being loud, soft, extremely uncontrolled, or still in

57

his presence does not make it holy

It is only acceptable if he has approved it as a reasonable sacrifice unto him.

> **Romans 12:1** *I beseech you therefore, brethren, by the mercies of God, that ye present your bodies a living sacrifice, holy, acceptable unto God, which is your reasonable service.*

We are quick to say that we do not engage in witchcraft, we do not serve idol Gods, we would never bow down to any other God. Yet to God, offering up strange incense is adultery, which to him is the serving of another God. When we yield to another God, even in error or ignorance, to God, it is idolatry. To serve idols is witchcraft.

> **Romans 6:13** *Neither yield ye your members as instruments of unrighteousness unto sin: but yield yourselves unto God, as those that are alive from the dead, and your members as instruments of righteousness unto God.*

> ➢ The word *Members* actually mean *"criminal intercourse."*
> ➢ *Unrighteousness* means *"violating law and justice or committing a wrongful act."*
> ➢ *Sin* means *"to err, to make a mistake, or miss the mark."*

The challenge with offering up strange fire when igniting revival is, rather than judging and gutting out witchcraft and idolatry in the land; strange fire strengthens it. Demons do not care if your intent was to sacrifice it to God. They are opportunists and it being strange gives them legal right to claim it as worship unto themselves. Whether we intended to be inappropriate in our worship or not does not matter. If God deems it a violation of his law or what he deems just – righteous - to him it is a criminal act that violates intimacy. To God, it is criminal intercourse, but to the devil it is acceptable intercourse. This is the reason those who offered up strange fire died (**Numbers 3:3-4, 2Samuel 6:6-7**). There desires, wills, and actions took precedence over God's standard. They end up being magnified as an idol god rather than serving and exalting the only true and living God.

We think because we are not dropping dead, God is pleased with what we present to him, or that he is pleased with how we officiate his glory. It is important to examine the fact that if we are striving to ignite revival, but there is minimal to no transformation in the people and the region, are we experiencing some form of spiritual death? What we consider a mighty awakening, God may consider strange. Strange equals no change or minimal change. Strange equals constant toiling and redoing the work with no or minimal progress. No change equals stagnation. Stagnation equals death. Minimal change does not represent the fullness of salvation. We, therefore, must stop settling and accepting minimal transformation and begin making the necessary changes to truly see an awakening in the earth.

This revelation of worship must be taught to revivalists, the team, to ministries, and to people as they unite with the revival awakening. It must be planted and plowed at every event. It would also be beneficial to have worship and fine arts intensives to teach, train and equip people to be liberated praise and worshippers. We do the people and the region an injustice to attend events, and they are not taught the standards and requirements of Godly worship. We fear offending people, or having them feel like we are judging their worship. Yet we allow all kinds of strange fire to be offered up and claim God is receiving it. We also resort to experiencing and only receiving a measure of breakthrough, because of the mixture of pure and strange worship being release into the atmosphere and the region. If people had a true revelation of how to worship God and how to come before God in worship without all the conditions, qualms, religious quirks, sin, strange fire, controlled worship, etc., MY GOD! What a powerful SHIFT of God that would be. It would be easier to ignite and solidify revival in people and regions.

It is time out for just having good shouting and emotional orgasmic worship - we feel good but are not fully transformed. We must teach people how to SHIFT and operate in the power of worship. We must teach people to enter in to God's presence where they:

- Receive deliverance from demonic strongholds, such that the powers of darkness are annihilated as they contend for breakthrough.
- Hear the voice of Lord and commune in Spirit to Spirit dialog with Jesus.
- Receive Revelation and strategies from the Lord.
- Journal and record what God is saying so they can be obedient to it in their daily lives.
- Receive miracles and healing in their bodies, souls, minds, new organs, body systems, limbs, bones, blood, cells, etc.
- Ignite deliverance and healing for others as they pray inside the glory of God and break others free; send the delivering word of God and heals others.
- Soak in the presence of God so he can heal and refresh them.
- Rest in the presence of God just to be with him and build further relationship with him.

- Pursue more of God so they can go higher and deeper in his Spirit, in relationship with him, and in elevating in dimensional SHIFTS in him.
- Experience supernatural encounters where they translate and operate in spiritual realms; visit heaven and bring heaven to earth.
- Operate in the spiritual realms where they contend and overthrow witches, warlocks, and principalities, powers and ruler spirits.

There are people who have special realms of authority in these areas, but this is the inheritance of every believer. Every believer can learn how to operate in these dimensions of worship where miracles, signs, and wonders flow continuously in the body of Christ. Equipping the believer in this area is essential to igniting eternal revival fire in the region. **SHIFT!**

CULTIVATING THE SUPERNATURAL

There are some revelations, warfare, and encounters that we can only have if we SHIFT to heaven and operate in spiritual realms.

> **Revelations 4:11** *After these things I looked, and behold, a door standing open in heaven, and the first voice which I had heard, like the sound of a trumpet speaking with me, said, "Come up here, and I will show you what must take place after these things."*

This heavenly position is our rightful inheritance and is one we should live through.

> **Ephesians 2:6** *"And hath raised us up together, and made us sit together in heavenly places in Christ Jesus."*
> *We seek to dance from the heavenly realms and not from the earth realm.*

The word *sit* denotes an actual position of authority, a throne, a place of rulership. Not only are we seated in heavenly places, but we are seated inside of Jesus, so he is our literal throne, our literal seat of authority. Often, when I am praying, I not only see myself sitting in Jesus, I am going deeper in him. I learned that as I go deeper in Jesus, other realms are being opened to me. The deeper I SHIFT through my seat in Jesus, the greater my authority, governmental rule, and dominion are over demons and the earth. This also allows me to maintain my posture of operating from my heavenly authority, as I am established in the kingdom and spiritual matters of God rather this world.

> **Colossians 3:1-4** *If ye then be risen with Christ, seek those things which are above, where Christ sitteth on the right hand of God. Set your affection on things above, not on*

things on the earth. For ye are dead, and your life is hid with Christ in God. When Christ, who is our life, shall appear, then shall ye also appear with him in glory.

The word *affection* means to *"entertain, interest or heart desires."* Everything we want and need should be in alignment with the kingdom of heaven. This is what revelation revivalists and revival ministries need to have so that they continuously seek to go higher and deeper in God. They must have a constant pursuit of the glory of God. They should never build a high place on their experiences no matter how mighty they are, as this will stifle his revival glory. God is infinite, therefore there are no limits to how far we can SHIFT in him. Revivalists have great favor for SHIFTING dimension and dimension in the glory of God.

Psalm 113:4-6 The LORD is high above all nations; His glory is above the heavens. Who is like the LORD our God, Who is enthroned on high, Who humbles Himself to behold The things that are in heaven and in the earth?

Psalms 147:5 Great is our Lord and abundant in strength; His understanding is infinite.

1Kings 8:27 But will God indeed dwell on the earth? Behold, heaven and the highest heaven cannot contain You, how much less this house which I have built!

Isaiah 40:28 Do you not know? Have you not heard? The Everlasting God, the LORD, the Creator of the ends of the earth Does not become weary or tired His understanding is inscrutable.

Romans 11:33 Oh, the depth of the riches both of the wisdom and knowledge of God! How unsearchable are His judgments and unfathomable His ways!

WHEWWWW! There is no limit to the depth of the SHIFT we can experience in Jesus. WHEWWWW! It is vital that revivalists and revival ministries live through this revelation, inheritance, and mantle. Living from your heavenly seat will enable you to govern the realms and heavenlies over your region. This is imperative to being able to discern principalities and powers and to assert authority and victory over the enemy.

Satan, the prince of the power of the air (*Ephesians 2:2*), understands the importance of operating in heavenly places.

> *1Peter 5:8 Be sober, be vigilant; because your adversary the devil, as a roaring lion, walketh about, seeking whom he may devour.*

Satan and his kingdom roam about the earth and in and out of heavenly realms seeking whom he can devour. Satan came to heaven one day, and God asked him where he had been.

> *Job 1:7 And the Lord said unto Satan, Whence comest thou? Then Satan answered the Lord, and said, From going to and fro in the earth, and from walking up and down in it.*

Satan understands that the power he needs to assert authority over the earth comes from exploring and governing from supernatural realms. Yet in the body of Christ, many of us talk about being supernatural, but we tend to operate from earth – the first heaven, which hoping the third heaven – the kingdom of God, will just reign down on us. I believe Satan and his kingdom set up rank in the second heaven, because we as God's people, did not and have not asserted our right to have and govern those realms. This is interesting in this day and time where many saints are conducting ministry on social media. Social media platforms are atmospheric gateways to supernatural realms. Even as we are releasing the gospel of Jesus Christ in these realms, we must war, guard, and displace principalities and powers, if we are going to eternally solidify the work that we are doing in these realms.

As we live a lifestyle from our heavenly seat, we must learn to yield to the Holy Spirit, so we can be translated and move about in spiritual realms. From a little child, I would have demonic visitations as I slept and in my dreams. And though I am now able to govern this through the leading of the Holy Spirit, from my youth my spirit would automatically astral project itself in the spirit realm. I did not understand that this was a gift and how to govern it until I was in my 30's. Before then, I dreaded this gift because witches, warlocks, and demons would see the light of God around me and would automatically attack me. In my 20's, I really begin to live for God, but no one around me understood my experiences and often contended I was demonically oppressed or had open doors. No matter how much deliverance and healing I received, these experiences did not cease. And because I was growing in God, they became more intense as demons, witches, and warlocks, would track me back to my home via the spirit realm and attack me further.

It was not until I attended a deliverance workshop by Apostle Ivory Hopkins, a general of balanced deliverance, that I received revelation that this was a gift due to my destiny and calling and that instead of trying to receive deliverance, I needed to ask the Holy Spirit to teach me how to operate in the gift and in spiritual realms. This revelation changed my life. I begin to seek strategy from the Holy Spirit. He began to give me revelation on the purpose of the gift and how though it was my inheritance to be seated in heavenly places with Christ Jesus, I had jurisdiction in these realms to combat principalities and powers, judge witches and warlocks, destroy high places. I am also able to acquire intel on the enemy's camp, and the Lord gives me strategy on how to defeat the enemy in people's lives, the land, atmospheres, climates, and regions. The devil and witches knew this, so when they saw me, they would jump me. Because I was ignorant to this, I was unaware I was in a war and a warrior. I was being beat up when I should have been towering. Help Lord!

I believe the psychiatric ward is full of mentally ill people who have a gift like mines but because the church does not operate in spiritual realms, they think and have been labeled as crazy and unstable. There have been plenty of times I have felt crazy and mentally challenged. I did not understand what was happening to me and seeking help from the saints only cofounded my oppression. I have had so many people speak hurtful things to me, make me feel belittled, demonized, filthy, and often when I sought help, the attacks would get worse. One time, I had a preacher tell me I was married to a demon, and he went through to procedure of performing a divorce ceremony on me. I realized that what was being spoken over me was further opening demonic spiritual doors where I was exposed to demons in spiritual realms.

I shared my testimony to state that we have authority in these realms. They belong to us, and we must claim and govern them, or the enemy will take up residence in our inherited territory.

It is important to note that the earth consists of three heavens:

1. The natural/physical realm is the first heaven.

2. The sky that we can see along with the galaxies, spheres, and realms that we cannot see with the natural eye, is the 2nd heaven.
3. The kingdom of God is the third heaven. The third heaven as all authority of the first and the second heaven.

The second heaven is where principalities and powers, witches and warlock, wicked and ignorant people who desire power and fame operate. These are the realms that govern the first heaven. It is also important to note that there are spiritual realms under the earth and in the waters.

Psalms 104:26 There the ships move along, And Leviathan, which You have formed to sport in it.

Psalms 55:15 Let death seize upon them, [and] let them go down quick into hell: for wickedness [is] in their dwellings, [and] among them.

Isaiah 27:1 In that day the LORD will punish Leviathan the fleeing serpent, With His fierce and great and mighty sword, Even Leviathan the twisted serpent; And He will kill the dragon who lives in the sea.

Ezekiel 26:16 Then all the princes of the SEA shall come down from their thrones, and lay away their robes, and put off their broidered garments: they shall clothe themselves with trembling; they shall sit upon the ground, and shall tremble at every moment, and be astonished at thee.

Luke 16:23 And in hell he lift up his eyes, being in torments, and seeth Abraham afar off, and Lazarus in his bosom.

Romans 8:37-39 Nay, in all these things we are more than conquerors through him that loved us. For I am persuaded, that neither death, nor life, nor angels, nor principalities, nor powers, nor things present, nor things to come, Nor height, nor depth, nor any other creature, shall be able to separate us from the love of God, which is in Christ Jesus our Lord.

Philippians 2:10 That at the name of Jesus every knee should bow, of things in heaven, and things in earth, and things under the earth;

Revelation 20:14 Then Death and Hades were thrown into the lake of fire. This is the second death, the lake of fire.

Revivalists and revival ministries must be cognizant of these realms and even ask for the eyes of their understanding to be enlightened on what realms wickedness is attacking the region from, and for strategy on how to combat them. It is also essential for revivalists and revival ministries to be offensive when dealing with demons, wickedness, and supernatural realms. If you are going to ignite revival, you cannot wait for demons to attack. Demons are already at work which is the entire reason we need revival. Do not wait until they increase their attack to assert authority over them. When asking God for a strategy to ignite revival fire, ask him for a strategy on how to govern in the supernatural. Practice living, making decisions, ministering, and governing from your heavenly seat, so you can continuously assert authority in every sphere of influence God grants to your hands.

Ask God to connect you with the seers in the region who can aide you in seeing into and guarding these realms. Ask God for discernment on what to do with what they share. Also ask for confidence not to fear and be intimidated by what they share, as God is always greater than the enemy. I see and have a keen knowing in spiritual realms. I see things that would make scary movies look like cartoons. I rarely share what I see because the average person would be horrified. But God gives me strategies and keys that I can share with people without frightening anyone. Even with sharing the strategy, I am the frontliner in implementing the revelation. Revivalists and leaders in the body of Christ, in general, must start training themselves and others to handle this information, so that supernatural realms become less spooky spiritual and where those who are called to contend can complete frontline ministry when they receive strategy. We want our realms to be our normal where we break the powers of demons and awaken revival glory in the earth.

JESUS! THE GREATEST REVIVAL WEAPON

Jesus is the name above every name. He is the name that every knee must bow. He is the way, the truth, and the light. He is the only way to salvation.

> ***Philippians 2:8-12*** *And being found in fashion as a man, he humbled himself, and became obedient unto death, even the death of the cross. Wherefore God also hath highly exalted him, and given him a name which is above every name: That at the name of Jesus every knee should bow, of things in heaven, and things in earth, and things under the earth; And that every tongue should confess that Jesus Christ is Lord, to the glory of God the Father.*

> ***John 14:6*** *Jesus saith unto him, I am the way, the truth, and the life: no man cometh unto the Father, but by me.*

> ***Acts 16:30-31*** *And brought them out, and said, Sirs, what must I do to be saved? And they said, Believe on the Lord Jesus Christ, and thou shalt be saved, and thy house.*

> ***Romans 10:9-10*** *If you declare with your mouth, "Jesus is Lord," and believe in your heart that God raised him from the dead, you will be saved. For it is with your heart that you believe and are justified, and it is with your mouth that you profess your faith and are saved.*

Demons bow, tremble, and are cast out at the name of Jesus.

> ***Matthew 7:22*** *On that day many will say to me, 'Lord, Lord, did we not prophesy in your name, and cast out demons vin your name, and do many mighty works in your name?'*

Matthew 17:27 And if I cast out demons by Beelzebul, by whom do your sons cast them out? Therefore they will be your judges.

Mark 16:17 And these signs will accompany those who believe: bin my name they will cast out demons; they will speak in new tongues;

Luke 10:17 The seventy-two returned with joy, saying, "Lord, even the demons are subject to us in your name!"

Acts 19:13 Then some of the itinerant Jewish exorcists undertook to invoke the name of the Lord Jesus over those who had evil spirits, saying, "I adjure you by the Jesus whom Paul proclaims."

James 2:19 Thou believest that there is one God; thou doest well: the devils also believe, and tremble.

Jesus is our greatest revival asset and weapon because he is revival. He is the entire reason we are to ignite revival in the earth. He must be at the center of our regional awakening.

Revelations 19:10 And I fell at his feet to worship him. But he said to me, "See that you do not do that! I am your fellow servant, and of your brethren who have the testimony of Jesus. Worship God! For the testimony of Jesus is the spirit of prophecy."

By testifying and proclaiming Jesus, we release the spirit of prophecy to activate future workings of his goodness, blessings, deliverance, healing, favor, salvation, prosperity, and protection. Because Jesus is the name above every name, and the name to which every knee bows, the more we exalt, proclaim and testify of him, the higher we SHIFT into supernatural realms with him.

John 12:32 And I, if I be lifted up from the earth, will draw all men unto me.

Lifted in this passage is *hypsoo̅* and means to
1. to raise to the very summit of opulence (wealth, riches, or affluence, abundance, as of resources or goods; plenty) and prosperity
2. to exalt, to raise to dignity, honor and happiness

A summit is the highest point of attainment or aspiration. When we lift Jesus up, his identity creates a pivotal clearing, such that we are SHIFTED out of our current spiritual or natural state, or from any bondages, oppressions depressions and possessions, to new governmental – diplomatic - dimension in him.

The very lifting of who he is as Lord judges people, the land, atmospheres, climates, and regions. The proclamation of his identity fills the heavens and the earth, and his very power and truth infuses the fruit of salvation into our sphere. The glory light of his nature also shines on the hidden - pushing it to the forefront where it is exposed, judged, and dispelled, as he continues to overtake everything with his existence.

> *Jeremiah 23:24 Can any hide himself in secret places that I shall not see him? saith the LORD. Do not I fill heaven and earth? saith the LORD.*

> *Zephaniah 3:17 The Lord thy God in the midst of thee is mighty; he will save, he will rejoice over thee with joy; he will rest in his love, he will joy over thee with singing.*

Because there is such mixture, idolatry, and blatant witchcraft in regions, we must be clear in making sure we identify and exalt the name of Jesus. During a mission's trip, I learned the importance of strategically identifying the name of Jesus, as opposed to even just saying God. I was with a team in Trinidad. Many of the people in the service claimed to be Christians, but they worshipped idol gods. Hinduism was potent in the nation, so it was not uncommon for people to have 30 to 100 or more gods. During the first night of ministry, when I would just say God, witchcraft would fill the atmosphere, and the worship would begin to sound like chanting to idol gods. I also would see principalities drawing the people unto themselves and securing their grip upon them. The Holy Spirit unction me to start declaring Jesus and to use the name Jesus Christ as opposed to saying God. When I did this, a clearing would occur in the spirit realm, demons manifested, and people would begin to get free of demonic strongholds. I learned that people, devils, hell, the land, climate, atmosphere, and region, need to know we are glorifying Jesus Christ – the name that is above every name. The proclamation of his name, who he is as savior, the power of his blood, and testifying of his gospel and goodness, is essential to regional awakening.

Furthermore, we must be mindful of how the displacement of people, principalities, and territorial spirits due to the rise of natural disasters such as hurricanes, tornados, tsunamis, fires, earthquakes, and even the trials of human trafficking, legal and illegal immigration, are impacting regions. Our regions are being infused with more witchcraft and idolatrous practices that America is not accustomed to. Yet because our nation respects everyone's right to worship the god of their choosing, the practices, beliefs, customs, and demon strongholds have free course in our regions. The regions in America have a lot of witchcraft shops, stores, restaurants that are really overt high places, where a lot of witchcraft spells, sacrifices, and idol worship are conducted. Many of us receive services in these businesses with no regard to what is being released over our food, clothing, etc.

Some of these businesses have idolatrous statues and pictures in plain sight. They have incense burning to idol gods. Some of us have an unction that something is off, yet we still trade and spend our money on these demonic floors. When we engage in this behavior, we are not exalting the name of Jesus in our region; we are strengthening and empowering demonic gods.

If we are going to have true revival eternally burning in the region, it is essential that we lift Jesus up in our everyday lives as well as in our events. We should exalt and proclaim him in our homes, in endeavors and situations, with our very presentation, disposition, and actions. We have to hate the things Jesus hates and love the things Jesus loves (*Psalms 97:10, Proverbs 6:16-19*). It is paramount to that we love Jesus with our very beings, where we deny anything that does not testify of him.

> *Matthew 22:37-38 Jesus said unto him, Thou shalt love the Lord thy God with all thy heart, and with all thy soul, and with all thy mind. This is the first and great commandment.*

> *Acts 17:28 For in him we live, and move, and have our being; as certain also of your own poets have said, For we are also his offspring.*

As a regional revivalist and gatekeeper, I am constantly bellowing out the name of Jesus as I walk through my home, in my car, in my personal prayer, and praise and worship time. Sometimes I just yell his name and let his name clear all the darkness and pressures of the enemy that tries to come at me. My region is strongly rooted in witchcraft, so I remain conscious of judging witches, warlocks, and their wickedness. I declare my region belongs to Jesus and I fall out of agreement with anything that does not LIFT HIM UP!

I declare that Jesus is the center of your revival awakening even now. I declare we are SHIFTING to a new dimensional altitude in understanding Jesus as revival, and him being our greatest asset to igniting and contending for revival in our region. **SHIFT!**

DISMANTLING BRASS HEAVENS

Deuteronomy 28:23 And thy heaven that is over thy head shall be brass, and the earth that is under thee shall be iron.

Brass is *hset* in the Hebrew and means:
1. copper, steal, bronze, metal
2. filthiness, lust, harlotry
3. dubious (of doubtful quality or propriety)
4. of uncertain outcome, wavering or hesitating in opinion

Haggai 1:10 Therefore the heaven over you is stayed from dew, and the earth is stayed from her fruit.

1Kings 17:1 Now Elijah the Tishbite, who was of the settlers of Gilead, said to Ahab, "As the LORD, the God of Israel lives, before whom I stand, surely there shall be neither dew nor rain these years, except by my word."

When the heavens are stayed or void of dew, it is:

Restricted	Prohibited	Reframed	Shut up
Held back	Forbidden	Withheld	Finished
A Drought	Famine	Dying of Crops	No Life or Reviving

There can be various reasons for a stayed or brass heaven. Some of these I will address, and some of them are self-explanatory or will be examined in other areas of the book.

➤ Sin, transgressions, and generational curses.

➤ Judgment from God due to sin.

➤ Principalities, powers, and territory spirits ruling the heavenlies.

➤ Lack of revelation, honor, and relationship with Jesus and the Holy Spirit.

➤ Witchcraft prayers and spells, binding the crossroads of the regions. Witches engage in these behaviors several times a year. They assert their authority over the four corners of the region by releasing a witchcraft spell around it and set a crossroad over the top of it, so they can bind the region to their control. They are fervent in locking down the territory because they understand the power of having the region under their control. After learning this, my ministry has been fervent with physically going to the center of our city:

- Breaking these witchcraft spells.
- Binding the prince of the power of the air over our region
- Commanding the demonic prince to remain eternally bound or to displace himself.
- Repenting and cleansing out the witchcraft spells released in the region.
- Releasing prayers that lock the region under the government of God.

I encourage revivalists and revival ministries to implement this strategy. You will experience a significant authority and greater ease of contending for revival if you implement it.

➤ Witchcraft clogging and controlling the portals of the region. Sometimes witches and warlocks will use the portals of the saints to astral project into spiritual realms and transact witchcraft tasks in the spirit. Especially, if we have allowed things into our sphere that open the doors to sin and yielding legal ground of the enemy. There are also instances where witches, warlocks, and demons will use your portal to track you. Whatever the case, I have found it beneficial to:

- Cleanse and fill the portal over my home, ministries, and region with the blood of Jesus and close off any entryways witches and demons are gaining access to my portals.
- I decree that my portals are connected to the throne room of God, and release the blood of Jesus from my sphere to the throne of God. Demons and witches hate the purity of the blood, and they hate the judgment of God's throne. They will stop using your portals if the blood of Jesus is there to judge and torment them.
- I release blindness and judgment to witches and demons, and decree amnesia and a zapping to information they know about me.

Your portals are gateways. Be mindful of this and be mindful of what you entertain in your sphere. When you are a revivalist, the enemy is looking for anyway to snuff out your fire. Be mindful to repent quickly, cleanse, and close doors to engaging in anything that gives him and his imps access.

➤ Lack of God ordained or responsible watchmen at the regional gate.

➤ The season for things needing to die in the ground and atmosphere.

➤ Lack of cultivation and contending for an open heaven. The heavens have to be cultivated. Constant prayer, praise and worship, declaration of scriptures, declarations and prophetic words, promises, affirmations, and the exaltation of Jesus are necessary to maintain an open heaven. Depending on the mantle your life and the region you live in, you may have to keep music, scriptures, and declarations playing in your home, ministry, and business to further assert continuous authority over your portals of heaven. This may sound like a bit much, but there are some idolatrous religions that offer up prayers and incense to their god 24 hours a day, and higher voodoo priests to keep the demonic altars burning for them and their families. The saints of God must grasp the power of consistency in lifting up Jesus where he effortlessly reigns in your sphere of influence.

➢ Strange fire versus pure praise and worship.

➢ Demonic Spirits of religion, tradition, and legalism causing a blanket or wall of suffocation and death within the atmosphere of people, ministries, and the region. These strongholds snuff out and block the spirit of God from flowing freely. They love to linger in services and conference and fine a way to quench the Holy Spirit from operating. The heavens will be wide open, then something will go sideways, and there will be like a literal choking of the presence of God in the spirit realm. There are times where my team and I have experienced this choking physically when ministering. The spirit realm becomes dark and hard as the heaven's close, and we will begin to cough, and choke as these spirits wrap themselves around our necks. It is essential to recognize when the presence of God is waning, or the heavens are closing, and examine if it is God led or if you have been snuffed out by religion and tradition. As you are cultivating revival, it is important to take time to deal with these spirits when they operate. Break their grip, hammer down their walls, and exalt Jesus until the heavens reopen, and darkness is push back. Many ministries will recognize this is happening but do nothing. When you do nothing, the ground you just conquered in the spirit, is now being overtaken by demonic spirits. You must recognize you are in a battle for territory. You have the ultimate authority to reign and govern in that sphere. Demons and wickedness can only reign if you slack in claiming your rightful inheritance.

As a revivalist, you initially cultivate an open heaven over your own life and home, and then you SHIFT into the region once you begin to maintain a consistent open heaven in your sphere. This will be training ground for contending with principalities and powers and will give you greater authority as you SHIFT into operating in your regional revival vision. It is important to understand that as a revivalist, you serve as a holy principality and have rank to contend with and overthrow principalities and powers. I have heard many ministers say you need a troop of saints to contend and displace principalities and powers. Biblically I have yet to come across a scripture to confirm that as truth. While we are waiting to gather believers to fight with us, principalities and territorial spirits are releasing all kinds of havoc into our lives. They are beating us up in our home, sleep, ministries, businesses, etc. I stand on *Luke 10:19,*

> *Behold, I give unto you power to tread on serpents and scorpions, and over all the power of the enemy: and nothing shall by any means hurt you. '*

I remain fervent in being offensive by seeking the Holy Spirit for enlightenment on what demonic forces are seeking to attack me and with discerning demonic activity. Whether it is a little devil or big devil, I invite Jesus, the angels, and the host of heaven to fight with me, and I beat devils down. Do not to be afraid to go a few rounds with a demonic power. Remember you are already victorious; if your victory is not manifesting, ask God for a strategy to contend for breakthrough. Implement that strategy until victory manifests. These types of experiences always teach you something, and empower you with more endurance, perseverance, and authority, to annihilate the enemy as you continue to SHIFT in your destiny and revival vision.

If you believe you do not have enough authority to contend with a demonic entity, then at least bind it up and prevent it from operating until others stand and pray with you. Do not just let demonic forces run rampant in your life out of fear, intimidation, or some religious rule of error.

> *Matthew 16:19 And I will give unto thee the keys of the kingdom of heaven: and whatsoever thou shalt bind on earth shall be bound in heaven: and whatsoever thou shalt loose on earth shall be loosed in heaven.*

When you sense something is clogging the heavens and is resisting your authority, you can ask God to rend the heavens with his revival fire and blast down on the devil.

> *Isaiah 64:1-3 The Amplified Version - Oh, that You would rend the heavens and that You would come down, that the mountains might quake and flow down at Your presence – As when fire kindles the brushwood and the fire causes the waters to boil – to make Your name known to Your adversaries, that the nations may tremble at Your presence! When You did terrible things which we did not expect, You came down; the mountains quaked at Your presence.*

The Message Version - *Oh, that you would rip open the heavens and descend, make the mountains shudder at your presence––As when a forest catches fire, as when fire makes a pot to boil––To shock your enemies into facing you, make the nations shake in their boots! You did terrible things we never expected, descended and made the mountains shudder at your presence.*

A rending is a violent tearing of the heavenlies. You have a right to ask God to tear the heavens, because Jesus already tore the veil, therefore, you have full access to the throne of God. Nothing should be separating you.

Matthew 27:50-51 Jesus, when he had cried again with a loud voice, yielded up the ghost. And, behold, the veil of the temple was rent in twain from the top to the bottom; and the earth did quake, and the rocks rent.

Ephesians 3:9-12 And to make all men see what is the fellowship of the mystery, which from the beginning of the world hath been hid in God, who created all things by Jesus Christ: To the intent that now unto the principalities and powers in heavenly places might be known by the church the manifold wisdom of God, According to the eternal purpose which he purposed in Christ Jesus our Lord: In whom we have boldness and access with confidence by the faith of him.

You can stand in this scripture and watch the Lord judge principalities on your behalf. But remember it requires bold faith as rending is a supernatural act and request for deliverance. God wants you to have access to his kingdom just as much as you want it for yourself. Trust him to honor you and to judge demonic powers on your behalf.

BREAKING UP THE FALLOW GROUND

Psalm 63:1-5 O God, you are my God; earnestly I seek you; my soul thirsts for you; my flesh faints for you, as in a dry and weary land where there is no water. So I have looked upon you in the sanctuary, beholding your power and glory. Because your steadfast love is better than life, my lips will praise you. So I will bless you as long as I live; in your name I will lift up my hands. My soul will be satisfied as with fat and rich food, and my mouth will praise you with joyful lips.

When we are cultivating and establishing revival in a region, we must contend from the ground just as we do the heavenlies. It is so important that we:

✓ Cleanse the land of past and present sin, famines and transgressions and break generational strongholds off the land (***Numbers, 14:18, Exodus 5:20, Jeremiah 2:6, Deuteronomy 28, Deuteronomy 32:10, Leviticus 26:38-42, Job 2:20, Ezekiel 20:5, Ezekiel 39, Haggai 1:10 Galatians 3:15***)

✓ Break up the hardness (***Hosea 10:12, Deuteronomy 8:23***)

✓ Cleanse waste and sickness from the land (***2Chronicles 7:14, Exodus 15:26, Micah 4:2, Matthew 4:15-16, Exodus 23:25, Revelations 22:2, 2Kings 2:19-21***)

> *Deuteronomy 28:21-23 The Lord shall send upon thee cursing, vexation, and rebuke, in all that thou settest thine hand unto for to do, until thou be destroyed, and until thou perish quickly; because of the wickedness of thy doings, whereby thou hast forsaken me.*

The Lord shall make the pestilence cleave unto thee, until he have consumed thee from off the land, whither thou goest to possess it. The Lord shall smite thee with a consumption, and with a fever, and with an inflammation, and with an extreme burning, and with the sword, and with blasting, and with mildew; and they shall pursue thee until thou perish. And thy heaven that is over thy head shall be brass, and the earth that is under thee shall be iron.

✓ Judge and displace demonic squatters and strongholds binding the land (***Ephesians 6:12, Luke 11:20, Matthew 12:28, Matthew 10:8, Matthew 18:18***)

✓ Judge demonic principalities and strongholds that may be lodge under the ground and under the waters (***Ephesians 6:10-12, Philippians 2:10, Matthew 10:8, Matthew 18:18***)

✓ Judge witches, warlocks, and demonic altars; Cleanse witchcraft and "destroy the high place. Do not be a "*good saint*" that shares the land with witchcraft as this grieves God. Do not allow them to remain in the land (***Exodus 22:18, Leviticus 20:6, Leviticus 6:27, Leviticus 26:30, Numbers 33:52, Jeremiah 7:31, 1Kings 3:2-3, 2Kings 15:3-4, 2Kings 23:8, Micah 5:10-12, 2Chronicles 34:3, Isaiah 8:19-22, Acts 19:17-20***)

✓ Claim Godly authority and jurisdiction over the land (***Genesis 1:27-28, Psalms 8:6, Hebrews 2:8***)

✓ Sow the kingdom and glory of God into the land (***Mark 1:15, Galatians 6:7-8, 2Corinthians 9:6, Matthew 13***)

- ✓ Reveal the unveiled glory instilled in the land.
  - *Isaiah 6:3 And one cried unto another, and said, Holy, holy, holy, is the LORD of hosts: the whole earth is full of his glory.*

  - *Numbers 14:21 But as truly as I live, all the earth shall be filled with the glory of the LORD.*

- ✓ Plow the womb of the land and region so it can be revived and fertile (**2Kings 2:18-22, Isaiah 54:1, Galatians 4:27, Psalms 127:5, Psalms 113:9**)

- ✓ Spiritually cultivate the land with the with words, decrees, purposes, plans of the Lord, so it can begin to transform into Godly land (**Genesis 3:18, Exodus 32:25-26, Deuteronomy 11:14-15, Job 22:28, 2Chronicles 20:20, Isaiah 41:18, 1Corinthians 5:17**).

- ✓ Train and equip the people to be land and business owners (**Exodus 6:8, Deuteronomy 6:10, Deuteronomy 30:20-21, Matthew 5:5**)

- ✓ Train the people to establish the kingdom of God every place the soles of their feet tread (**Deuteronomy 1:4, Joshua 1:3**)

To implement the strategy above, we must first break up the iron and fallow ground.

Deuteronomy 28:23 And thy heaven that is over thy head shall be brass, and the earth that is under thee shall be iron.

Iron means the ground is:

Harsh	Stronghold	Rigid	Ruthless
Oppressed	Cruel	Robust	Unbending
Shackled	Immovable	Stubborn	Unyielding

Hosea 10:12 Sow to yourselves in righteousness, reap in mercy; break up your fallow ground: for it is time to seek the LORD, till he come and rain righteousness upon you.

The Message Version Sow righteousness, reap love. It's time to till (break up) the ready earth (the fallow Ground), it's time to dig in with God, Until he arrives with righteousness ripe for harvest.

Fallow means the ground is:

Untilled	Unplowable	Stale	Hard
Uncultivated	Depleted	Fruitless	Neglected
Unseeded	Dry	Infertile	Undeveloped
Inactive	Empty	Sterile	Untilled
Unattended	Spiritually Void	Parched	Vacant
Unplanted	Impoverished	Waste	Virgin
Slacked	Impotent	Asleep	Neglected

That is so sad. HELP US GOD!

Figure 4DryLand Picture from yessweeterthanhoney.wordpress.com

Though our regions appear to be plowed in the natural, spiritually the ground of many of our regions are fallow.

The fact that much of our natural plowing lack sufficient production to keep our regions healthy, successful, stable, and progressive is also proof of the spiritual fallow grounds in our regions. Seeming that most of our regions are consumed with demonic and worldly systems, laws, morals, and standards, yields further revelation that the spiritual ground of our regions is fallow.

You know how some houses or buildings catch on fire, but after the fire, the structure of the house or building is still standing? We do not want that. We want everything to be consumed in the revival fire, so everything that is not of God is burned up and everything that is of him remains, is refined, transformed and is equipped for effective use beyond the fire. We want to break up the fallow ground in our lives, families, ministries, lands, and regions.

> *Hebrews 12:27-29 And this word, Yet once more, signifieth the removing of those things that are shaken, as of things that are made, that those things which cannot be shaken may remain. Wherefore we receiving a kingdom which cannot be moved, let us have grace, whereby we may serve God acceptably with reverence and godly fear: For our God is a consuming fire.*

To break up the fallow ground, revivalist, revival ministries, and the people must cultivate a lifestyle of righteousness. As we are imputed to righteousness, we must become penetrable where the revival fire consumes us, becomes us, such that we are plowable and surrendered for God to work through us as a righteous seed infusing the earth.

As righteousness is used to break up the iron and fallow ground, it releases:

Rightness	Virtue	Justice	Righteous acts
Rectitude	Prosperity	Judgment	Righteous Government

Our righteousness has to be a literal seed of judgement fire and hammer when breaking up the ground.

Jeremiah 23:9 Does not my word burn like fire?" says the LORD. "Is it not like a mighty hammer that smashes a rock to pieces?

Holman Christian Standard Bible *"Is not My word like fire"--this is the LORD's declaration--"and like a hammer that pulverizes rock?*

Dictionary.com defines *pulverize* as:
1. to reduce to dust or powder, as by pounding or grinding
2. to demolish or crush completely
3. to defeat, hurt badly, render helpless

When God wreaks righteous judgment on the ground, he has no mercy.

Revelation 21:8 *But the fearful, and unbelieving, and the abominable, and murderers, and whoremongers, and sorcerers, and idolaters, and all liars, shall have their part in the lake which burneth with fire and brimstone: which is the second death.*

Genesis 19:24-25 *Then the Lord rained upon Sodom and upon Gomorrah brimstone and fire from the Lord out of heaven; 25 And he overthrew those cities, and all the plain, and all the inhabitants of the cities, and that which grew upon the ground.*

We must be like our Father when it comes to releasing righteous judgment on the land. We cannot have any mercy.

Along with interceding, purging, waring, judging, overtaking, decreeing and declaring, we must also be righteous foot soldiers upon the land.

- We should be evangelizing the land.
- We should be establishing businesses, ministries, organizations, etc., in the land.
- Though we have a launching post where we train, equip, and host events, we should also have events all over the region to aide in expanding the heavens, overtaking the ground, and igniting revival all over the land.
- We should be cultivated as righteous seeds, so when we go about our daily lives, we instill the consuming revival fire of God in the land.
- We need prophetic foot soldiers in our services who are warring and contending over the land. They must have a governmental jurisdiction and understanding of the need to not just plow the atmosphere and heaven, but the land.
- We need frontline foot soldiers established during praise and worship that can go before the praise and worship team and the people to clear the land so that revival can take up residence in the land. Dance ministers are frontline foot soldiers. They must be trained in their calling, honored and partnered into the revival vision. I will discuss this in more detailed in this next chapter as dance ministers are essential for revival being eternally solidified in the earth. Without the dance ministers in place, we risk constantly toiling, while demons and wicked people continue to take back the land from us because we do not have dance ministers in position to guard the gates of the land. COME ON! **SHIFT!**

BENEFITS OF FINE ARTS MINISTRY

Fine Arts Ministry (FAM) arsenals peculiar weapons that are significant in igniting revival and keeping the glory and kingdom of God burning in a region.

> **2Corinthians 10:4-6** (*For the weapons of our warfare are not carnal, but mighty through God to the pulling down of strong holds;) Casting down imaginations, and every high thing that exalteth itself against the knowledge of God, and bringing into captivity every thought to the obedience of Christ; And having in a readiness to revenge all disobedience, when your obedience is fulfilled.*

Weapons are the instruments, tools, armor, artillery, arsenal, weaponry, of God for the purposes of making us offensive for war.

Warfare is *strateia* in the Greek and means:
1. military service, i.e. (figuratively) the apostolic career (as one of hardship and danger)
2. an expedition, campaign, military service, warfare
3. metaph. Paul likens his contest with the difficulties that oppose him in the discharge of his apostolic duties, as warfare

When we engage in praise and worship, we are indeed in a war.

> **Psalms 149:6** *Let the high praises of God be in their mouth, and a twoedged sword in their hand; To execute vengeance upon the heathen, and punishments upon the people; To bind their kings with chains, and their nobles with fetters of iron; To execute upon them the judgment written: this honour have all his saints. Praise ye the Lord.*

High Praises means *"to uplift, to exalt, arise."* When high praises go forth, we are sounding an alarm that causes an uprising. We are being lifted into another dimension with God, God is being lifted up, and the kingdom of heaven is being lifted to contend with anything that is against God.

One of the dictionary's definitions of *arise* is to *"rise in revolt."* When we rise in revolt we:

- ❖ Break away from or rise against constituted authority
- ❖ Become open rebellion
- ❖ Cast off allegiance or subjection to those in authority
- ❖ Rebel and incite mutiny
- ❖ Turn away in mental rebellion, utter disgust, or abhorrence

Our posture of ministry should be appalled and disgusted about anything that is against God while releasing FAM that contends and overthrow darkness.

> *Psalms 100:4 Enter into his gates with thanksgiving, and into his courts with praise: be thankful unto him, and bless his name.*

Courts is an actual place of judgement and justice.

The devil knows we are in a battle as he lives his life roaming seeking whom he may devour. He and his camp hears the alarm we are sounding when we go forth in praise and worship and as we minister through our fine arts giftings.

Whether we acknowledge it or not, when we sound our alarm, we enter into contention with any principalities and powers that do not want to give up their jurisdiction in the heavenlies around us, and against any strongholds that do not want to release the people.

It is important that dance ministers, psalmist, musicians, revivalists, revival ministries, recognize this war is occurring, so they can be mindful of not just cultivating their little church atmosphere, but taking up spiritual residence in communities and regions.

> *1Corinthians 1:27 But God hath chosen the foolish things of the world to confound the wise; and God hath chosen the weak things of the world to confound the things which are mighty.*

FAM encompasses foolish weapons that confounds, baffles, discombobulates, stifles, damns, defeats, the demons, demonic powers, wickedness, and prideful people that think they know God or think that they are above God.

- Dance is the movement and embodiment of the word, presence, and purpose God.
- Song is the voice, melody, harmony, musicality, emotions, mind, and expressed ideas of the word, presence, and purpose of God.
- Music and Instruments are the sound, frequencies, radiance, rhythm, flavor, vibration, sovereign character and governmental authority of the word, presence, and purpose of God.
- Poetry and paintings reveal the creativity, visionary, heart, and clarity of the word, presence, and purpose of God.

  - Dance materializes the physical manna of God.
  - Song vocalizes the laws, standards, and nature of God.

- Music controls the airways with the infusion and rulership of the kingdom of God
- Poetry and paintings visually imprint and establish God's existence in the earth.

2Corinthians 3:18 But we all, with open face beholding as in a glass the glory of the Lord, are changed into the same image from glory to glory, even as by the Spirit of the Lord.

As God is unveiled and implanted through FAM, people, atmospheres, climates, etc., are transformed into the likeness of God and his Kingdom.

Matthew 6:10 Thy kingdom come. Thy will be done in earth, as it is in heaven.

In order to fully comprehend the benefits and power of FAM, we must ascertain that God has an arsenal of weapons that he has released from heaven.

Jeremiah 50:25 New Living Translation The LORD has opened his armory and brought out weapons to vent his fury. The terror that falls upon the Babylonians (my regions and sphere of influence) will be the work of the Sovereign LORD of Heaven's Armies.

King James Bible The LORD hath opened his armoury, and hath brought forth the weapons of his indignation: for this is the work of the Lord GOD of hosts in the land of the Chaldeans.

The Amplified Bible The Lord has opened His armory and has brought forth [the nations who unknowingly are] the weapons of His indignation and wrath, for the Lord God of hosts has work to do in the land of the Chaldeans.

The Lord has a work to do in regions. He has released FAM as weapons of his indignation and wrath against the works of darkness.

Dictionary.com defines *indignation* as:
1. strong displeasure at something considered unjust
2. offensive, insulting, or base; righteous anger

Dictionary.com defines *wrath* as:
1. strong, stern, or fierce anger; deeply resentful indignation; ire
2. vengeance or punishment as the consequence of anger

Fine art ministers must be utilized so they can rise up with indignation and wrath regarding the strongholds that are striving to beset the people and your community. They must be honored and released to arise with stern displeasure and fierce anger against the killings, poverty, lack idolatry, perversion, debauchery, legalism, racism that is plaguing our regions.

Those around them must arise in the revelation that every time they dance, sing, play an instrument, release poetic utterance, paint, they are a weapon of mass destruction released to judge and destroy the enemy.

> **Isaiah 13:4-5** *The noise of a multitude in the mountains, like as of a great people; a tumultuous noise of the kingdoms of nations gathered together: the Lord of hosts mustereth the host of the battle. They come from a far country, from the end of heaven, even the LORD, and the weapons of his indignation, to destroy the whole land.*
>
> **Isaiah 5:26** *And he will lift (banner) up an ensign to the nations from far, and will hiss unto them from the end of the earth: and, behold, they shall come with speed swiftly:*

<u>*Hiss* is *saraq* in the Hebrew and means to:</u>
to be shrill, i.e. to whistle or hiss (as a call or in scorn)

> **New International Bible:** *He lifts up a banner for the distant nations, he whistles for those at the ends of the earth. Here they come, swiftly and speedily!*

> **Isaiah 10:5** *O Assyrian, the rod of mine anger, and the staff in their hand is mine indignation.*

> **New International Bible** *Woe to the Assyrian, the rod of my anger, in whose hand is the club of my wrath!*

> **Jeremiah 50:15** *Shout against her round about: she hath given her hand: her foundations are fallen, her walls are thrown down: for it is the vengeance of the LORD: take vengeance upon her; as she hath done, do unto her.*

<u>*Shout* is *rua* in the Hebrew and means:</u>
1. to split the ears, to raise or signal a battle cry
2. to sound and alarm, destroy, triumph

Fine art ministers must work together and value one another. Work together because:
- Your shout of dance and drama
- Your shout of song
- Your shout of sound
- Your shout of poetry
- Your shout of portrait illustration

May encompass what is needed to destroy in triumph over the enemy.

> **1Samuel 1:27** *"How have the mighty fallen, And the weapons of war perished!"*

This is the reason we must understand that
- ✓ We are all one body with different parts
- ✓ We must value one another's gifts and mantles
- ✓ We must not embrace and empower one another in our giftings and callings

We never know what weapon we are negating when we reject the gifts and callings of our brother or sister in Christ. They may be the very weapon we need to save lives, takeover land, transform regions. I DECREE A SHIFT TODAY IN BEING UNIFIED AND HONORING ONE ANOTHER IN THE LORD!

PSALMIST MINISTRY
Since songs release the laws, standards, and nature of God, it is important to release prophetic songs, spiritual songs, melodies, decrees, and utterances that aligns with the vision of revival and what you are seeking to ignite in the people, land, and the region during your services.

> **Ephesians 5:19** *Speaking to yourselves in psalms and hymns and spiritual songs, singing and making melody in your heart to the Lord;*
>
> **Colossians 3:16** *Let the word of Christ dwell in you richly in all wisdom; teaching and admonishing one another in psalms and hymns and spiritual songs, singing with grace in your hearts to the Lord.*

Many of these songs are produced spontaneously through the Spirit of God as:

Spiritual Songs in the Hebrew is *pneumatikos* and is defined as:

96

1. non-carnal, i.e. (humanly) ethereal (as opposed to gross), or (demonically) a spirit (concretely), or (divinely) supernatural, regenerate
2. religious, spiritual, belonging to the divine spirit of God, or a being higher
3. one who is filled with and governed by the Spirit of God, pertaining to the wind or breath

The great power of spiritual songs is that they are new songs. And we know new is the essence of revival. As they are ministered, they are releasing the refreshing and reviving thoughts, will, purpose, heart, and intent of the Lord. Spiritual songs are birthed out of the spirit of God; therefore, people, lands, and regions are receiving the literal breath of God. It is as if God is breathing life and revival into people, land, and region, from his very being. If the psalmist is not living a life rooted in God, what they are singing can be sinful and/or demonically induced, and therefore they are releasing the spirit of carnality and/or demons into the people.

Psalm 33:1-3 Sing for joy in the Lord, O you righteous ones; praise is becoming to the upright. Give thanks to the Lord with the lyre; sing praises to Him with a harp of ten strings. Sing to Him a new song; play skillfully with a shout of joy.

Psalm 95:1 O come, let us sing for joy to the Lord, let us shout joyfully to the rock of our salvation.

Psalm 96:1-2 Sing to the Lord a new song; sing to the Lord, all the earth. Sing to the Lord, bless His name; proclaim good tidings of His salvation from day to day.

Psalm 98:1 O sing to the Lord a new song, for He has done wonderful things, His right hand and His holy arm have gained the victory for Him.

Psalm 100:1-2 Shout joyfully to the Lord, all the earth. Serve the Lord with gladness; come before Him with joyful singing.

Psalm 147:1 Praise the Lord! For it is good to sing praises to our God; for it is pleasant and praise is becoming."

Psalm 149:1 Praise the Lord! Sing to the Lord a new song, and His praise in the congregation of the godly ones.

Spiritual songs enable the revival awakening to remain in the fresh flow of the Lord while releasing the fresh word and fresh radiance of the Lord. Psalmists who operate in spiritual songs are strategically producing *"a new thing."* They instill a regenerating fiery anointing upon the people, the land, and the region, that judges and annihilates death and produces the miracles, signs, and wonders.

MINSTREL MINISTRY (Minstrel excerpt from my "God's Shifting Power" Book)

Music is armor the produces transforming SHIFTING sounds:

*2Chronicles 5:13-14 It came even to pass, as the trumpeters and singers were as one, to make one sound to be heard in praising and thanking the Lord; and when they lifted up their voice with the trumpets and cymbals and instruments of musick, and praised (**halal act like a mad man**) the Lord, saying, for he is good; for his mercy endureth for ever: that then the house was filled with a cloud, even the house of the Lord; So that the priests could not stand to minister by reason of the cloud: for the glory of the Lord had filled the house of God.*

Instruments is *kliy* in the Hebrew and means:
1. vessel, weapon, jewel, ware

2. armor bearer, armor, furniture, utensil article,
3. implement (of hunting or war) implement (of music)
4. implement, tool (of labor)
5. equipment, yoke (of oxen)

Musicians are able to govern the atmosphere through sound:

> *Psalms 67:3-7 Let the people praise thee, O God; let all the people praise thee. O let the nations be glad and sing for joy: for thou shalt judge the people righteously, and govern the nations upon earth. Selah. Let the people praise thee, O God; let all the people praise thee. Then shall the earth yield her increase; and God, even our own God, shall bless us. God shall bless us; and all the ends of the earth shall fear Him.*

Praise in this scripture is *yada* and means:
1. to use (hold out) the hand; physically, to throw (a stone, an arrow) at or away
2. especially. to revere or worship (with extended hands)
3. intensively, to bemoan (by wringing the hands), cast (out), (make) confess, confession, praise, shoot, (give) thanks, thanksgiving
4. to cast, cast down, throw down
5. to confess, confess (the name of God)

Judge is *sapat* in the Hebrew and means:
1. to judge, pronounce sentence (for or against), to vindicate or punish
2. by extension, to govern; passively, to litigate (literally or figuratively)
3. avenge, that condemn, contend, defend, execute (judgment), (be a) judge, judgment, needs, plead, reason, rule, defend, deliver,
4. govern, vindicate, punish

5. to act as law- giver or judge or governor (of God, man)
6. to rule, govern, judge to decide controversy

> *The Amplified Bible Let the peoples praise You [turn away from their idols] and give thanks to You, O God; let all the peoples praise and give thanks to You. O let the nations be glad and sing for joy, for you will judge the peoples fairly and guide, lead, or drive the nations upon earth. Selah [pause, and calmly think of that]! Let the peoples praise You [turn away from their idols] and give thanks to You, O God; let all the peoples praise and give thanks to You! The earth has yielded its harvest [in evidence of God's approval]; God, even our own God, will bless us. God will bless us, and all the ends of the earth shall reverently fear Him.*

> *The Message God! Let people thank and enjoy you. Let all people thank and enjoy you. Let all far–flung people become happy and shout their happiness because you judge them fair and square, you tend the far–flung peoples. God! Let people thank and enjoy you. Let all people thank and enjoy you. Earth, display your exuberance! You mark us with blessing, O God, our God. You mark us with blessing, O God. Earth's four corners––honor Him!*

Sounds dismantle principalities and strongholds:

When sounds govern adequately, it causes principalities and strongholds to collapse. It dismantles the fortified strongholds of the enemy and exposes his kingdom.

> *Joshua 6:20 So the people shouted when the priests blew with the trumpets (as giving a clear sound): and it came to pass, when the people heard the sound of the trumpet, and the people shouted with a great shout, that the wall*

fell down flat, so that the people went up into the city, every man straight before him, and they took the city.

The Message Bible *The priests blew the trumpets. When the people heard the blast of the trumpets, they gave a thunderclap shout. The wall fell at once. The people rushed straight into the city and took it.*

Blew is *taqa* in the Hebrew and means:
1. to clatter, slap (the hands together), clang (an instrument)
2. to drive (a nail or tent- pin, a dart, etc.)
3. to become bondsman by hand clasping, blow (a trumpet), cast, clap, fasten, pitch (tent), smite, sound, strike, thrust
4. to give a blow, blast, to thrust, drive (of weapon) to give a blast, give a blow to strike or clap hands
5. to be blown, blast (of horn), to strike or pledge oneself

When sound governs adequately it makes demons manifest and exposes soulish issues:

2Samuel 6:15-16 So David and all the house of Israel brought up the ark of the Lord with shouting, and with the sound of the trumpet. And as the ark of the Lord came into the city of David, Michal Saul's daughter looked through a window, and saw King David leaping and dancing before the Lord; and she despised him in her heart.

Sounds gathers the people in unity for war:

Nehemiah 4:19-20 The Amplified Bible And I said to the nobles and officials and the rest of the people, the work is great and scattered, and we are separated on the wall, one far from another. In whatever place you hear the sound of the trumpet, rally to us there. Our God will fight for us.

The Message Bible *Then I spoke to the nobles and officials and everyone else: "There's a lot of work going on and we are spread out all along the wall, separated from each other. When you hear the trumpet call, join us there; our God will fight for us."*

Psalms 47:5-7 *God is gone up with a shout, the Lord with the sound of a trumpet. Sing praises to God, sing praises: sing praises unto our King, sing praises. For God is the King of all the earth: sing ye praises with understanding.*

Amplified Bible *God has ascended amid shouting, the Lord with the sound of a trumpet. Sing praises to God, sing praises! Sing praises to our King, sing praises! For God is the King of all the earth; sing praises in a skillful psalm and with understanding.*

The Message Bible *Loud cheers as God climbs the mountain, a ram's horn blast at the summit. Sing songs to God, sing out! Sing to our King, sing praise! He's Lord over earth, so sing your best songs to God.*

Aramaic Bible in Plain English *God went up in glory! Lord Jehovah with the sound of the trumpet!*

<u>*Praises* in this scripture is *zamar* and means:</u>
1. the idea of striking with the fingers); properly
2. to touch the strings or parts of a musical instrument
3. play upon it; to make music, accompanied by the voice
4. to celebrate in song and music, give praise, sing forth praises, psalms

Sound in the Hebrew is _qol_ and means:
1. to call aloud; a voice or sound
2. sound aloud, bleating, crackling, cry (out)
3. fame, lightness, lowing, noise, hold peace, (pro-) claim, proclamation
4. sing, sound, +spark, thunder, thundering, voice, yell

Sound is atmospheric, and it triggers the response of the Lord:

The louder the sound, the greater God is exalted and the bigger he becomes. As he increases, his judgment is released in our midst.

> _Psalms 149:5-9 Let the high_ **(romma which means exaltation, uplifting, arising)** _praises of God be in their mouth, and a twoedged sword in their hand; To execute vengeance upon the heathen, and punishments upon the people; To bind their kings with chains, and their nobles with fetters of iron; To execute upon them the judgment written: this honour have all his saints. Praise ye the Lord._

Sounds raise the dead and has the ability to release a quick work for God:

What could take years can occur in a twinkling of an eye with the correct sound. Spiritual sound thus dispels death and darkness and produce miracles. They SHIFT things from the corrupt and temporal to the eternal. Sounds SHIFT us into the very nature and essence of our eternal God.

> _1Corinthians 15:52-54 In a moment, in the twinkling of an eye, at the last trump: for the trumpet shall sound, and the dead shall be raised incorruptible, and we shall be changed. For this corruptible must put on incorruption,_

and this mortal must put on immortality. So when this corruptible shall have put on incorruption, and this mortal shall have put on immortality, then shall be brought to pass the saying that is written, Death is swallowed up in victory. O death, where is thy sting? O grave, where is thy victory?

Amplified Bible In a moment, in the twinkling of an eye, at the [sound of the] last trumpet call. For a trumpet will sound, and the dead [in Christ] will be raised imperishable (free and immune from decay), and we shall be changed (transformed). For this perishable [part of us] must put on the imperishable [nature], and this mortal [part of us, this nature that is capable of dying] must put on immortality (freedom from death). And when this perishable puts on the imperishable and this that was capable of dying puts on freedom from death, then shall be fulfilled the Scripture that says, Death is swallowed up (utterly vanquished forever) in and unto victory. O death, where is your victory? O death, where is your sting?

The Message Bible You hear a blast to end all blasts from a trumpet, and in the time that you look up and blink your eyes—it's over. On signal from that trumpet from heaven, the dead will be up and out of their graves, beyond the reach of death, never to die again. At the same moment and in the same way, we'll all be changed. In the resurrection scheme of things, this has to happen: everything perishable taken off the shelves and replaced by the imperishable, this mortal replaced by the immortal. Then the saying will come true: Death swallowed by triumphant Life! Who got the last word, oh, Death? Oh, Death, who's afraid of you now?

God requires fresh and new songs and sounds:

Psalms 149:1-4 Praise ye the Lord. Sing unto the Lord a new song, and his praise in the congregation of saints. Let Israel rejoice in him that made him: let the children of Zion be joyful in their King. Let them praise his name in the dance: let them sing praises unto him with the timbrel and harp. For the Lord taketh pleasure in his people: he will beautify the meek with salvation.

The Message Bible Hallelujah! Sing to God a brand-new song, praise him in the company of all who love him. Let all Israel celebrate their Sovereign Creator, Zion's children exult in their King. Let them praise his name in dance; strike up the band and make great music! And why Because God delights in his people, festoons plain folk with salvation garlands!

Often when the bible speaks of instruments, especially the trumpet, it speaks of giving a clear sound or a continuous sound as with the ram's horn:

1Corinthians 7-8 And even things without life giving sound, whether pipe or harp, except they give a distinction in the sounds, how shall it be known what is piped or harped? For if the trumpet give an uncertain sound, who shall prepare himself to the battle?

The Amplified Bible If even inanimate musical instruments, such as the flute or the harp, do not give distinct notes, how will anyone [listening] know or understand what is played? And if the war bugle gives an uncertain (indistinct) call, who will prepare for battle?

The Message Bible If musical instruments—flutes, say, or harps—aren't played so that each note is distinct and in tune, how will anyone be able to catch the melody and enjoy the music? If the trumpet call can't be distinguished, will anyone show up for the battle?

There is a strategic flow that is released in sound. This flow is necessary for moving in alignment with what God is desiring in a service.

> *John 7:38* *He that believeth on me, as the scripture hath said, out of his belly shall flow rivers of living water.*
>
> *The Amplified Bible* *He who believes in Me [who cleaves to and trusts in and relies on Me] as the Scripture has said, From his innermost being shall flow [continuously] springs and rivers of living water.*
>
> *The Message Bible* *Rivers of living water will brim and spill out of the depths of anyone who believes in me this way, just as the Scripture says.*

Flow is *rheo* in the Greek and means:
1. a prolonged form
2. used to flow ("run"; as water), flow

Rivers is *potamos* in the Greek and means:
1. a current, brook or freshet (as drinkable), i.e. running water
2. flood, river, stream, water, a torrent

There is a prolong flow and even a current that praise and worship should flow on and it should SHIFT us upward - upstream - as we should constantly elevate if we are on the correct current with God.

Dictionary.com describes *torrent* as:
1. a stream of water flowing with great rapidity and violence
2. a rushing, violent, or abundant and unceasing stream of anything
3. a violent downpour of rain

4.   a violent, tumultuous, or overwhelming flow

This means as we are on the correct current, there should be an abundance of rivers flowing from our belly and even down pouring upon us from the heavenlies.

> **Psalms 46:4** *There is a river (prosperity, flood), the streams whereof shall make glad the city of God, the holy place of the tabernacles of the most High*

> **Verse 4-5 The New English Translation** *A river brings joy to the city of our God, the sacred home of the Most High. God dwells in that city; it cannot be destroyed. From the very break of day, God will protect it.*

Waters usually represent the Holy Spirit, so this is a continuous flow of presence of God. Moreover, water suggests a cleansing, refreshing, drenching.

<u>*Waters* is Greek for *hydor* and means:</u>
1.   waters in rivers
2.   in fountains
3.   in pools of the water
4.   of the deluge of water
5.   in any of the earth's repositories
6.   of water as the primary element
7.   out of and through which the world that was before the deluge, arose and was compacted of the waves of the sea fig. used of many peoples

When waters flow things get swallowed up and drowned out. The fountains and the pools come to wash us from the old and make us new, wash us from the demonic and make us like God, refresh and empower us all the more in God.

Genesis 2:20 A river watering the garden flowed from Eden; from there it was separated into four headwaters.

Psalms 16:11 You make known to me the path of life; you will fill me with joy in your presence, with eternal pleasures at your right hand.

Psalms 23:2 He makes me lie down in green pastures, he leads me beside quiet waters,

Psalms 36:8 They feast on the abundance of your house; you give them drink from your river of delights.

Psalms 43:3 Send me your light and your faithful care, let them lead me; let them bring me to your holy mountain, to the place where you dwell.

If a person truly desires to operate in the SHIFTING sounds of a minstrel, it is very important to live a sanctified and holy life and be set a part for God.

The word "minstrel" in the Hebrew is *"nagan"* and means, *"to play or strike strings, sing to the stringed instruments, melody, player, to make music, beat the tune with the fingers."* From this definition alone, we discern that the anointing on a minstrel is one of warfare and using his or her giftings to strike blows against the enemy and his camp. Having open doors through unrepentant and blatant sin, only adds to the warfare and gives the enemy legal right to triumph and conquer over the minstrel. The minstrel must know that they are sound carriers, so whatever they subject themselves to is what flows and filters through the sounds he or she produces and releases. This is one of the reasons people are being emotionally stimulated but not truly transformed during church and ministry services.

Oftentimes, sound in praise and worship is contaminated by what the minstrel has subjected themselves to the outside of God's presence and will, so the sound released is not effective enough to shift and change someone's life. We may experience one or two miracles out of grace, but the full anointing of the Holy Spirit is not flowing in purity, so God cannot really operate in our contaminated midst. Churches and ministries have to not only govern the ministry but make minstrels accountable to the gifting and calling on their lives. The minstrel's lifestyle must be conducive to the nature and character of God so that God's sound can be produced with miracles, signs, and wonders.

David is our greatest example of a minstrel sold out for God. God described him as a man after His own heart and one who followed His commandments. Because David had a heart for God, he produced anointed and skillful sounds that brought deliverance even to his enemies shifted atmospheres and gave him favor with people and with God.

> *1Samuel 13-14 But now thy kingdom shall not continue: the LORD hath sought him a man after his own heart, and the LORD hath commanded him to be captain over his people, because thou hast not kept that which the LORD commanded thee.*

> *Acts 13:22 After removing Saul, he made David their king. God testified concerning him: 'I have found David son of Jesse, a man after my own heart; he will do everything I want him to do.'*

> *1Samuel 16:22 And it came to pass, when the evil spirit from God was upon Saul, that David took an harp, and played with his hand: so Saul was refreshed, and was well, and the evil spirit departed from him.*

1Samuel 18:7 And the women answered one another as they played, and said, Saul hath slain his thousands, and David his ten thousands.

David was prophetic and apostolic. David prophesied regarding Jesus Christ *(Psalm 22:16; Psalm 16:10; Isaiah 53:10-11; Psalm 68:18; Psalm 110:1)*

We also know of bible stories of how he consistently prophesied and established God's kingdom through praise, song, dance, war, declaration, and music. The bible also reveals David's apostolic ability to SHIFT and transform himself, people, and atmospheres through his minstrel anointing.

DANCE MINISTRY

While much of the fine arts weapons are atmospheric, dance ministers are atmospheric and ground pulverizing ministers. They are foot soldiers who break up the fallow ground *(Hosea 10:12)* and deal with demonic strongholds in the land and under the ground of the region while taking up the ground for the kingdom of God. King David was a dancing foot soldier. In *2Samuel 6:13-16*, as the Levite priest properly bared the ark of the covenant, David danced before God with all his might and offered sacrifices, which enabled the ark of the covenant to be successfully restored into its rightful place in the region of Israel.

2Samuel 6:13-16 And it was so, that when they that bare the ark of the Lord had gone six paces, he sacrificed oxen and fatlings. And David danced before the Lord with all his might; and David was girded with a linen ephod. So David and all the house of Israel brought up the ark of the Lord with shouting, and with the sound of the trumpet. And as the ark of the Lord came into the city of David, Michal Saul's daughter looked through a window, and saw king

David leaping and dancing before the Lord; and she despised him in her heart.

The Levi family of Korath were the revivalists of their day. They were the only ones authorized to carry the glory. They carried the glory on staves, placed upon shoulders (*Study Num. 3:30-31; 4:15; 7:9; Exod. 25:14-15*). Earlier in *2Samuel 6*, the ark was being carried on a cart driven by oxen.

> *2Samuel 6:6-7 And when they came to Nachon's threshingfloor, Uzzah put forth his hand to the ark of God, and took hold of it; for the oxen shook it. And the anger of the Lord was kindled against Uzzah; and God smote him there for his error; and there he died by the ark of God.*

In trying to prevent the ark from falling, Uzzah touched the ark and dropped dead. This violated **Numbers 4:15**, where if the holy things are touched, the penalty is death. The cart nor Uzzah was an authorized glory carrier. The revival glory cannot be carried just any old way or by just anybody.

The Levites bearing the Ark of the Covenant upon their shoulders insinuates that there is a great obligation, oppression, responsibility, and accountability in making sure that the task is done with precision, excellence, integrity, and righteousness. It is as if that calling or task is weighing down upon the revivalist. They are humbled up under the pressure - the weight - the weighty *Kabod* glory of the ark (*Kabod* is the Hebrew word for weighty glory).

As David brought the Ark of the Covenant to Israel the second time, he was careful to bear it the way God designed and even implemented a strategic plan of dancing and offering a sacrifice unto the Lord every six paces.

<u>*Sacrifice*</u> in this passage of scripture is *zabah* and means:

111

1. to slaughter an animal (usually in sacrifice): — kill, offer
2. to (do) sacrifice, slay, offer
3. to slaughter for sacrifice, to slaughter for eating, to slaughter in divine judgment

Dancing is a treading weapon.

> **Joshua 1:3** *Every place that the sole of your foot shall tread upon, that have I given unto you, as I said unto Moses.*

<u>Tread in the Hebrew is *dârak* and means:</u>
1. to tread; by implication, to walk; also to string a bow (by treading on it in bending)
2. an archer, which is someone who shoots with a bow and arrow
3. bend, come, draw, go (over), guide, lead (forth), thresh, tread (down),
4. treader, tread upon, lead, march, march forth

> **Luke 10:19** *Behold, I give unto you power to tread on serpents and scorpions, and over all the power of the enemy: and nothing shall by any means hurt you.*

<u>Tread is *Pateo* in the Greek and means</u>
1. to trample, crush with the feet, to advance by setting foot upon, tread upon
2. to encounter successfully the greatest perils from the machinations and persecutions with which Satan would fain thwart the preaching of the gospel
3. to tread under foot, trample on
4. to treat with insult and contempt
5. to desecrate the holy city by devastation and outrage

Through his dance, David was judging and trampling to contempt, anything in the land and region that was disobedient or contrary to God's will. David sacrificed the very thing he had carried the ark upon when Uzzah died; he sacrificed oxen along with fatling. Oxen are prideful, bullheaded, stubborn animals. Fatlings are grossly engorged, manmade fattened, domineering animals. David made it clear before God, the people, the land, and the region, that carrying the Ark of the Covenant in this manner was an error. Through the sacrificing of oxen and fatlings, he was humbling himself unto God's purpose and standards, while cleansing, ridding, and killing strange fire and everything his actions and the actions of others had instilled in the land that would defy God.

It is great that we have those in the congregation that will praise, shout, and dance in services. However, we need God ordained, set apart, mantled dance ministers who understand how to properly judge the land and offer sacrifices of worship that cleanse, rid, and destroy disobedience, sin, and strange fire in the land. They go before the revivalists to protect the glory of God and to make the land holy and conducive for God to dwell and be established in the land.

Many ministry events have psalmist and musicians, but no dancer ministers in position. There tends to be an open heaven, but the ground is hard and impenetrable because there are no dance ministers to do war in the land. We are quick to encourage praisers from the audience to dance, and this is very essential. However, if they are not mantled Levites, they are just offering up worship unto God, but the strongholds in the land will not surrender to them, or they will relinquish for a moment, but when the worship stops, they regain control over the land. Dancers are frontline ministers who lead ministries and the people in war as praise and worship goes forth. They are able to tread and assert authority over the land, where God's purpose, presence, and kingdom is eternally solidified.

Many ministries, do not cultivate an appreciation for dance ministry, but this must change. We must understand that the devil will succumb to allowing us to have our open heaven, as long as what is being released from heaven, does not infuse and cause transformation in the land. The land is where the manifestation of heaven will truly reveal itself. When the land becomes conducive and fertile with heaven, it begins to produce the blessings and harvest of God's kingdom, where we begin to see personal and economic growth in the people and the regions. We begin to see the land and region SHIFT to looking like the inheritance of God.

THE REGION KNOWS MY NAME
Some of this revelation is from my,
"Sustaining The Vision Workbook."

Revivalists, fivefold ministry gifts, and ministries, in general, must understand that the region knows your name.

> *Isaiah 49:1-4 Listen, O isles, unto me; and hearken, ye people, from afar; The Lord hath called me from the womb; from the bowels of my mother hath he made mention of my name. And he hath made my mouth like a sharp sword; in the shadow of his hand hath he hid me, and made me a polished shaft; in his quiver hath he hid me; And said unto me, Thou art my servant, O Israel, in whom I will be glorified. Then I said, I have laboured in vain, I have spent my strength for nought, and in vain: yet surely my judgment is with the Lord, and my work with my God.*

> *New Living Translation Listen to me, all you in distant lands! Pay attention, you who are far away! The Lord called me before my birth; from within the womb he called me by name. He made my words of judgment as sharp as a sword. He has hidden me in the shadow of his hand. I am like a sharp arrow in his quiver. He said to me, "You are my servant, Israel, and you will bring me glory." I replied, "But my work seems so useless! I have spent my strength for nothing and to no purpose. Yet I leave it all in the Lord's hand; I will trust God for my reward."*

We tend to think that being called means a plan has been set in our lives for the future, but *the Message Version* of this scripture reads:

> *The Message Version Listen, far-flung islands, pay*

115

attention, faraway people: God put me to work from the
day I was born. The moment I entered the world he
named me.

God put me and you to work from birth! We think destiny started when we became saved or when we begin doing something successful. It has been God's intentions that the call on our lives launched us into working for him from the day we left the womb.

The scripture says *"Listen, O isles, unto me; and hearken, ye people, from afar."* That word *isles* in the Hebrew means *region*. **Listen, O region!** That is a command or mandate proclamation. **Listen, O isles, O region!**

<u>*Listen* is *šâma* in the Hebrew and means:</u>
1.   to hear intelligently and to be obedient
2.   listen attentively, carefully, certainly
3.   to consent, declare, discern, or give ear
4.   to perceive, proclaim, publish, regard, report, to bear witness

The region has ears, and you can command it to listen intelligently. You can command it to be diligently obedient to what you are saying and to respond to what you are decreeing by mandating that it publishes your words while bearing witness by producing the fruit of your words in the region. As you decree into the region, the region declares back to you what you said by producing your words in the land, people, businesses, ministries, organizations, atmosphere, climate, and heavenlies. Or in your specific case, by producing your words concerning your destiny and vision into the earth. These are words that God has already published in the region as the word *call* is *qârâ'* in the Hebrew and means, *"the idea of accosting a person."* Accosting means, *"to confront boldly, to approach especially with a* greeting." *Qara* also means, *"to call out to (i.e. properly, address by name, to call forth, cry (unto), (be) famous, guest, invite, mention, (give) name, preach, (make) proclamation, pronounce, publish.*

The region knows we are called from birth because God released our destiny into the ears of the region when we were in the womb. He did not just speak it; he cried it out with proclamation such that once we are born, the region can respond to our destiny as we begin to journey in life with God. As God gives you goals, plans, visions, strategies, and decrees to speak and complete in the region, you are awakening his will and purpose that was placed in the region at your birth. How awesome is that?

Hearken is *qâšab* in the Hebrew and means:
1. to prick up the ears, to incline, attend (of ears)
2. to give heed, regard, pay attention, listen, give attention

After you command the region to listen, you can prick the ears of (hearken) the people or your remnant, or those who will gleam from your destiny within the region and command them to listen, regard, attend, pay attention, give attention to you and to what the region is producing through you. As you exalt God through decrees, intercession, and warfare regarding what you speak in the region, God being exalted causes those who need who you are and what you are producing to be drawn to you. It is very important to cleanse out atmospheres about you and just in general because whatever is spoken in that region the region listens, can hear it, and publishes that into its ground and sphere.

Romans 8:19 *declares "for the earnest expectation of the creature waiteth for the manifestation of the sons of God.*

117

The region is anxiously waiting on us, so it can manifest the depth of what God has put in it.

> **English Standard Version** *For we know that the whole creation has been groaning together in the pains of childbirth until now.*

We discern from this scripture that the region is a portal that constantly groans - constantly giving birth to our words, prayers, and declarations. The region is always in a birthing position. ***Genesis 1:28*** *declares "be fruitful and multiply."* This scripture is not just talking about birthing natural children, but about what can be birthed into regions. The region is always positioned to give birth and to multiply. The region is ready you as the revivalists, for you as the fivefold ministry, and for the revival, you are to awaken within it.

> **Isaiah 49:2** *And he hath made my mouth like a sharp sword; in the shadow of his hand hath he hid me, and made me a polished shaft; in his quiver hath he hid me;*

Sharp is *hadad* in the Hebrew and means *"to be fierce, to be alert, keen, piercing."* Since our mouths are sharp swords, it is a literal cutting instrument, a knife, dagger, an axe, or shall we say a weapon. A fierce, keen, piercing weapon. If God has hidden you in the shadow of his hand, then his hand is in front of you, and you are like an illusion behind his hand. As he has you hidden in his hand, he has made you like a polished shaft. A shaft is an arrow or staff. *Polished* means he has chosen you and prepared you for this work and to be a weapon in this region. What this means is, when we are operating in the region and spheres of influence that God has ordained for our lives, we have authority to tower in destiny and in the revival vision he has given us. When we are not in our proper region and sphere of influence, we endure a lot of warfare and hardship. We are striving to birth in a region that does not know us, and where God has not deposited anything about us that can be produced in our midst.

Many do not have or understand this revelation and tend to want to live or produce destiny where they desire with no regard to what God is saying. Even Jesus had a heart to minister and be a blessing in his home town, but the people lacked unbelief.

> **Matthew 13:53-58** *And it came to pass, that when Jesus had finished these parables, he departed thence. And when he was come into his own country, he taught them in their synagogue, insomuch that they were astonished, and said, Whence hath this man this wisdom, and these mighty works? Is not this the carpenter's son? is not his mother called Mary? and his brethren, James, and Joses, and Simon, and Judas? And his sisters, are they not all with us? Whence then hath this man all these things? And they were offended in him. But Jesus said unto them, A prophet is not without honour, save in his own country, and in his own house. And he did not many mighty works there because of their unbelief.*

Despite being born in this country, the region did not know Jesus' name. Also, the words that were associated with Jesus as savior were not published in the womb of the region. Therefore, instead of believing and having faith, the people and the region wreaked with unbelief. This hindered Jesus from being able to effectively produce in the lives of the people and in the region. He was also dishonored and despised, despite being a prophet and astounding the people with his teachings and wisdom. Rather than embrace him, they debased him as a carpenter's son and was offended by him. They did not see him as the savior of the world that he was called to be.

- ❖ You may be born in a city, but that may not be the place you are to journey in destiny or ignite revival.
- ❖ You may desire to live in a particular city, state, or nation, but make sure God wants you to live and ministry there.
- ❖ You may want to do online ministry, but if your name and destiny has not been published in those spheres, it may produce minimal fruit, or if it does produce fruit, it may not be unto the glory of God.
- ❖ You may want to minister, teach, etc., in a particular city, state, or nation, but make sure God has published your name there so you can have authority and perform many miracles, signs, and wonders for his glory.

Make you are releasing your revival blueprint in the region God has ordained. This ensures that you, those connected to your destiny, and the region, receives, produces, and establishes the kingdom and rule of heaven for God's glory.

GATEKEEPING INTERCESSION

It is vital that regional revivalists and revival ministries comprehend that they are gatekeepers. Gatekeepers are watchmen in charge of the regional gates. They must keep guard of the regional gates and identify fivefold ministry officers within their regions who have been called to guard the gates (*Ephesians 4:8-11*). Gatekeepers govern, cover, and protect the region, by guarding, monitoring, identifying, supervising, and judging, the traffic, and flow of what is allowed in and out of the region. Gatekeeper watch at the gate and through divine intercession, warfare, prophecy, declaration, divine utterance, and strategy, they control what goes in and out of the gate. They provide access or deny access to the region. If you are going to ignite revival in the region, you must govern the gates. Otherwise, the people and the region are sharing space with demonic bondage. You are working contrary to your revival mandate, as demonic or misplaced gatekeepers govern the traffic of the region while counterattacking, undermining, overriding, and dismantling your progress and stamina.

One of the revelations I received as one called to ignite revival and guard the gates in my region, is that I must pray for the region and guard the gates with the same fervency that I pray for my personal life. The region is intertwined in my identity and realm of influence. My life is not apart from it. As I pray daily for myself, I am also warring, interceding, cleansing, imparting, governing, covering, and protecting the region. This is vital because most people tend to wait until they gather with other believers to pray for the region and/or govern the gates. Or they pray for the region as they think about the importance of it. But as a regional revivalist, you are to consistently ignite revival fire at the gate. You are not waiting until you get with your prayer team, get to church, your ministry event, or waiting on a Holy Ghost unction. You recognize that the region is a part of your inheritance and mandate, and as you pray fervently for your life, you also pray for the region.

Though not always the case, many times, it is not the mega church in the region or the platformed minister that is called to awaken revival. Yet this ministry and minister is usually viewed as the gatekeeper among the religious arenas within the region. We must understand that the gatekeeper is not who we choose or deem worthy. They are not chosen by church numbers or notoriety. God chooses the gatekeeper. The revivalist cannot be intimidated to take his or her position at the gate if that is what God is saying. They must also connect with God ordained gatekeepers, so they can have an effective likeminded team governing the gates.

When religion, tradition, and legalism rule a region, often religious and legalistic ministers control the gates. They may be praying at the gates for the region, but they control what part of God is active in the region. This is one of the reasons the kingdom of God and the Holy Spirit does not reign in a region or is only operable in measure. Witches and warlocks understand the importance of guarding the gates of regions. They love power. They fast, engage in consistent demonic intercession and prayers, and offer sacrifices to idols, so they can receive rank and authority to govern the gates of the region. As a result, manmade doctrines and ideations, worldly systems, and demons control the region rather than God.

Continual fervent prayer and intercession for the people and the region are needed at the gates.

> *Psalms 24:7-17 Lift up your heads, O ye gates; and be ye lift up, ye everlasting doors; and the King of glory shall come in. Who is this King of glory? The Lord strong and*

mighty, the Lord mighty in battle. Lift up your heads, O ye gates; even lift them up, ye everlasting doors; and the King of glory shall come in. Who is this King of glory? The Lord of hosts, he is the King of glory. Selah.

We discern from this passage of scripture that the gates have ears, eyes, and heads. Gates are the head of the region. The gatekeepers in this passage had to be alarmed to arise in their rightful place as gatekeepers and greet the glory and might of the Lord. This reveals that some are at the gate, but are not on their watch. They have access to be gatekeepers but are not operating in their authority. And some may even be sleep at the gate, as **The Message Bible** reads:

Wake up, you sleepyhead city! Wake up, you sleepyhead people! King-Glory is ready to enter. Who is this King-Glory? God, armed and battle-ready. Wake up, you sleepyhead city! Wake up, you sleepyhead people! King-Glory is ready to enter. Who is this King-Glory? God-of-the-Angel-Armies: he is King-Glory.

The gatekeepers are placed at the gate to watch and intercede so that they may foresee the threats to the region. The gatekeepers were asleep; even though God wanted to enter in and bless the people, loathing had overtaken the region and put the city asleep. We tend to focus on the heavens over the region, but God is one of order, so even though the glory and kingdom of God appears to come from the heavens and even from different cardinal directions of the earth, it is the gatekeepers who sound the alarm, and give access for the glory and kingdom of God to come in. God submits himself to the gates and waits for access or alarms the gatekeepers to give him access, so he can enter in and work in the region.

There are protocols to govern the security of the gates. Depending on who governs the gates, these protocols may be reprogramed to meet the standards of the gatekeeper. If the gatekeeper is not Godly, then God's mandate will have a difficult time being established in the region. Often when we see breakthrough, it is because the gates were temporarily governed. Whether that be during a prophetic or warfare moment at an event, intercessory meeting, or church service. But because the revivalist or fivefold minister does not know this is their rightful place, and they are to live in the authority of a gatekeeper, while consistently governing the gate, the illegal gatekeepers retake control of the gates. It is vital that we stop this tug of war fight at the gates.

LIFT UP YOUR HEADS OH YE REVIVALISTS!
LIFT UP YOUR HEAD OH YE APOSTLES!
LIFT UP YOUR HEAD OH YE PROPHETS!

WE NEED YOU AT THE REGIONAL GATES! SHIFT!

REVIVAL REPENTENCE

A lifestyle posture of repentance is essential to igniting revival. Adam and Eve did not know sin, so they had no concept that they should have repented and even ask for mercy. They took on the nature of the devil when they sinned and made excuses for their actions rather than repent. This resulted in consequences being released rather than mercy.

Repentance is not just idle words or lip service to God. Revival ministers and ministries should be willing to stand in the gap and display a grieved heart for the generational sins of the people and the region. There must be a broken spirit and contrite heart for the past and present sins that have been committed in the land lives of the people, and atmosphere of the region.

> *Psalms 51:17 The sacrifices of God are a broken spirit: a broken and a contrite heart, O God, thou wilt not despise.*

Broken in this passage of scripture means *"crushed, destroyed, to rend violently, to wreck."* The demonstration of true repentance is a disposition of the heart that is displayed through a humble intercessory posture of mercy, but also through the physical lifestyle actions of a person's behavior.

> *2Chronicles 7:14 If my people, which are called by my name, shall humble themselves, and pray, and seek my face, and turn from their wicked ways; then will I hear from heaven, and will forgive their sin, and will heal their land.*

<u>Turn in the Hebrew is *sûb* and means:</u>
1. to turn back (hence, away) transitively or intransitively, literally or figuratively (not necessarily with the idea of

return to the starting point); generally, to retreat; often adverbial, again

2. break, build, circumcise, dig, do anything, do evil, feed, lay down, lie down, lodge, make, rejoice, send, take, weep)) again

3. (cause to) answer (+ again), bring (again, back, home again), call (to mind), carry again (back), cease, convert, deliver (again), deny, draw back

As we spend time crying out for repentance of personal and regional sins, those who are interceding must display Godly sorrow through their everyday living. Over the years, we have seen some revivals die with the exposure of sin conducted by those who were revivalists or due to sin and witchcraft creeping into the ministry. Many will say that the work was complete, and the Holy Ghost Fire was put out by God, but what glory does God receive from quenching revival? God wants the revival fire to never burn out. A revival should never end because of sin. Even if after a work has run its course, that revival fire should continue to manifest in whatever God is SHIFTING that revivalist or ministry to do next, as God is about advancing and progressing his kingdom, not quenching it. Revivalists and ministries must become examples of Godly living before the people and behind closed doors. Otherwise, revival will be quenched within the ministry and region as sin always kills revival.

People and ministries who desire to ignite revival must be mature in the following areas:

Holy fear and reverence for the Lord. People who wain in this area, abuse or live through erred principles of grace, have a propensity to yield to sin.

Proverbs 15:16 *Better is a little with the fear of the LORD Than great treasure and turmoil with it.*

Proverbs 22:4 *The reward of humility and the fear of the LORD Are riches, honor and life.*

Psalm 128:1-4 *How blessed is everyone who fears the LORD, Who walks in His ways. When you shall eat of the fruit of your hands, You will be happy and it will be well with you. Your wife shall be like a fruitful vine Within your house, Your children like olive plants Around your table. Behold, for thus shall the man be blessed Who fears the LORD.*

Luke 1:50 *And His mercy is upon the generation after generation toward those who fear him.*

A repenting heart and a mindset to repent quickly.

Acts 3:19 *Repent ye therefore, and be converted, that your sins may be blotted out, when the times of refreshing shall come from the presence of the Lord.*

A mindset to forgive quickly and live unoffendable.

Colossians 3:13 *Be even-tempered, content with second place, quick to forgive an offense. Forgive as quickly and completely as the Master forgave you.*

A hunger for the character, nature, and integrity of God and unwillingness to settle for any likeness that does not represent God.

2Corinthians 3:18 *But we all, with open face beholding as in a glass the glory of the Lord, are changed into the same image from glory to glory, even as by the Spirit of the Lord.*

A hunger and thirst for righteousness, holiness, purity, and virtue.

> **Matthew 5:6** *Blessed are they which do hunger and thirst after righteousness: for they shall be filled.*

> **Matthew 6:33** *But seek ye first the kingdom of God, and his righteousness; and all these things shall be added unto you.*

An unwillingness to bear fruit apart from God.

> **John 14:15** *Abide in me, and I in you. As the branch cannot bear fruit of itself, except it abide in the vine; no more can ye, except ye abide in me.*

> **John 15:15** *I am the vine, ye are the branches: He that abideth in me, and I in him, the same bringeth forth much fruit: for without me ye can do nothing.*

A practiced lifestyle of living on and through mindsets and attributes that will manifest the good report of the Lord.

> **Philippians 4:8-9** *Finally, brethren, whatsoever things are true, whatsoever things are honest, whatsoever things are just, whatsoever things are pure, whatsoever things are lovely, whatsoever things are of good report; if there be any virtue, and if there be any praise, think on these things. Those things, which ye have both learned, and received, and heard, and seen in me, do: and the God of peace shall be with you.*

> **Matthew 6:6** *One's private life must be conducive to one's spiritual life. But you when you pray, enter into your inner room, and having shut your door, pray to your Father, the One in secret. And your Father, the One seeing in secret, will reward you.*

These attributes are essential to not bringing reproach upon God by igniting a flame that our character and lifestyle cannot maintain. As revival cannot be hidden. If it is truly revival, it will draw lots of attention and crowds of people. Revivalist and ministries must be able to sustain in the work of the Lord as not to grieve the Holy Spirit and incite reproach upon the work of Lord when it results in the quenching of revival fire.

> **Ephesians 4:5** *And grieve not the holy Spirit of God, whereby ye are sealed unto the day of redemption.*

> **Philippians 2:15** *So that you will prove yourselves to be blameless and innocent, children of God above reproach in the midst of a crooked and perverse generation, among whom you appear as lights in the world, holding forth the word of life; that I may rejoice in the day of Christ, that I have not run in vain, neither laboured in vain.*

> **The Message Bible** *Do everything readily and cheerfully — no bickering, no second-guessing allowed! Go out into the world uncorrupted, a breath of fresh air in this squalid and polluted society. Provide people with a glimpse of good living and of the living God. Carry the light-giving Message into the night.*

DEMONIC OPERATIONS

To solidify revival fire in the region, it is important to know the ranks of demons, and their demonic and witchcraft operations. I will share some in this chapter, but encourage revivalists and revival ministries to ask God to reveal the witchcraft and demonic operations in your region, how they operate, and further study them, so you can equip yourself to contend and overthrow their workings.

> *Ephesians 6:12-13 For we wrestle not against flesh and blood, but against principalities, against powers, against the rulers of the darkness of this world, against spiritual wickedness in high places. Wherefore take unto you the whole armour of God, that ye may be able to withstand in the evil day, and having done all, to stand.*

Levels of Warfare

❖ **Ground Level Warfare** involves casting demons out of individuals, places, and things.

❖ **Occult Level Warfare** involves witchcraft, idolatry, or strategic organizations that are really powers of darkness, or spiritual wickedness in high places within a community or region. Examples, Freemasonry, Sororities, Fraternities, New Age Practices, Buddism, Tibetan, Yoga, etc.

❖ **Strategic Level Warfare** is where principalities and territorial spirits are assigned by Satan to directly bind, influence, and govern the activities of communities, regions, states, nations. They also coordinate demonic activities in political, governmental, economic, financial, educational, business, and entertainment arenas.

Demon Rankings

- **Demons** are demonic forces, evil spirits or devils that possess, depress, oppress, torment, influence, or stronghold a person place or thing. The manner in which these demonic spirits attack is as follows:

  - ❖ **Oppress** -to burden, restrain, weigh heavy upon, to put down; press down, subdue or suppress an atmosphere or the soul, heart, body of a person.

  - ❖ **Depress** – to make sad or gloomy; lower in spirits; deject, dispirit, to lower in force, vigor, activity, etc.; weaken, make dull, a person or atmosphere.

  - ❖ **Negatively influenced** – cause confusion, discombobulation, double mindedness, unexplainable weariness, tiredness or sluggardness, irritation, frustration, ungodly thoughts, thought racing within a person or atmosphere.

  - ❖ **Possess** – to occupy, dominate, or control a person or atmosphere

- **Strongholds** are demonically possessed, demonically depressed, demonically gripping clutches, barriers, fortresses, walls, or entanglements that harass, influence, hinder and/or prevent a person from being free to walk in the full salvation for the Lord (*2Corinthians 10:3-5, Ephesians 4:22-23, Matthew 16:19, Mark 3:27*).

- **Principalities** are satanic princes and territorial spirits ruling over a nation, city, region, and community for the purposes of establishing Satan's demonic plan in people lives and spheres.

- **Powers** are high ranking supernatural demons or demonic influences that cause evil and sin in the world.

- **Rulers of Darkness** are demonic forces that govern deception and manipulative hardships and catastrophes that are generally produced by witchcraft, manipulation of the weather and worldly systems; they operate in cultures and countries such that idolatry and sin reign in the earth.

- **Spiritual Wickedness in High Places** are evil plots and deceptions, and demonic attacks directed in and against the church and God's people for the purposes of hindering, contaminating and demolishing God's will in the earth.

Witchcraft Practices

Witchcraft is the practice of magic, especially black magic; it is the utilization of spells and the invocation of demons to bind people, families, ministries, businesses, organizations, land, atmospheres, climates, regions, nations. Some people engage in witchcraft for entertainment, curiosity, or due to ignorance. Those that dedicate their lives to it use it to acquire personal success and advancement, power, fame, rank in spiritual realms, spheres, to obtain high ranking positions and platforms in the natural.

Some witchcraft practices include:

Sorcery	Magic	Witching	Wizardry
Black Magic	White Magic	Candle Magic	Spells
Hexes	Vexes	Hoodoo	Voodoo

Wicca	Mojo	Chants	Demonic Crossroads
Santeria	Yoruba Religion	Hinduism	New Age Practices
Horoscopes	Tarot Readings	Psychic Readings	Chain Letters
Familiar Spirits	Spirit Guides	High Priest/Priestess	Demonic Omens
Necromancy	Yoga	Shamanism	Fortune Telling
Hypnotism	Acupuncture	Psychic Readings	Superstition
Reincarnation	Ouija Boards	Fengshai	Good Luck Charms
Buddhism	Tibetan	Freemasonry	Eastern Stars
Sororities/Fraternities	Psychic Readings	Witchery	Pagan Holidays
Chakras	Kundalini	Astrology	Tarot Cards
Numerology	Dream Catchers	Palm Readings	Fortune Cookies

There is no such thing as a good witch or good witchcraft. All witchcraft is bad and evil in nature. The Holy Spirit of God is the only good spirit. There is no such thing as a good demonic spirit. God does not desire us to use sorcery, spells, and demonic manipulation to influence anyone's life. Regardless of what perceived good, that manifests from witchcraft; its source is rooted in demonic spirits that have now become gateways and influencers in your life. These demonic spirits open doors for other demonic spirits to operate so that as bad things happen, other spirits come along and serve as perceived rescuers to keep people tied to the demonic entities. But all of this is so they can keep people as a spiritual host and gateway to them operating in the earth realm, as spirits need bodies to effectively complete their demonic assignments in the earth.

Please understand that witches, warlocks, and demons do not have people's best interest at heart. Witchcraft is rooted in self-absorbed, self-idolatrous gain, and so the witches and demons are always getting something out of it; whether that is influence, possession, demonic rank, or drawing the life source out of people into themselves for more, energy, power, and strength. We must judge these workings, demonic agents, and demonic forces in our region, so the people, land, and region can be delivered, healed, and set free.

It is important to note that witches and warlocks pray against ministries and leaders within their territory. They pursue information about who the gatekeepers are, and they spend countless hours sending spells, curses, and demonic assignments hinder, stifle, and kill the word of the Lord.

Sometimes they physically visit and release curses and incantations on the people, land, atmosphere, assignments of leaders and the ministries. In addition, they will astral project into homes, ministries, and regions to release curses, spells, and demonic assignments. They will even physically war, seek to intimidate, and afflict leaders, ministries, and visions as they project themselves through spiritual portals.

Witches tend to operate during the witching hours of 12am to 3am. They, however, will do their work all day and night for the purpose of inciting evil upon God's people and kingdom. They are committed to their assignments. We too must be fervent in our offense in canceling these attacks before they are released.

With the rising use of social media and the online web, witches, and warlocks spiritually map and track leaders and ministries through these means. They utilize the information as manipulators to release curses, spells, and demonic assignments. We must be careful what we release online. We must also be cognizant that the web has its own set of realms and influences. It is a global sphere. We must close off and thwart the attacks and assignments that are being unleashed through these portals and gateways.

I tend to declare that witchcraft works boomerang back upon the senders' own lives, families, and camps. There are instances I will send it back seven times stronger or destroy it and their kingdom all together. God was not passive with witchcraft in the bible, and he is not passive today (*Exodus 22:18*). These entities want to kill you and destroy God's people, work, and kingdom in the earth. Holy Spirit will lead you with how to combat these attacks. The key is to deal with them. They are the main reason many visions do not come to pass, never reach full maturity, or experience the level of fruit God intended for their lives and ministries.

❖ **Incantations** Are demonic spells released around people, homes, families, property, land, atmospheres, communities, regions, or whatever the witch/warlock desires to box someone in to their control and working. Incantations can even be done around a person's mind, heart, soul, and physical body for the

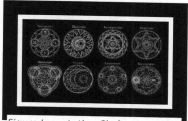
Figure Incantation Circles

purpose of manipulation and control. It will often

135

feel like you are boxed in or something is binding or wrapped around you personally, a particular area of your body, or around the area you are in. Often on TV, it will look like a circle, but this circle boxes you in where you are bound and cannot operate in their own strength or will, or the strength and will of God. Break the powers of the demonic circle/box and command it to loose whatever it has boxed in. Loose the blood of Jesus and fire of God to be a hedge of protection around the person, land, region, etc.

❖ **Ley Lines** are spiritual lines witches, and warlocks create with magic powers to hex people, land, and regions. They will release a line that has a spell on it and will place it somewhere that they know you will cross, such as a door, entryway, etc., and when you do, it activates the spell in your life. Witches are known for putting little trinkets, salt lines, cursed bibles and artifacts on the doors of minister's houses and ministries, and when they connect with them or cross those lines, it activates a spell in their life. Be mindful of this as when you begin to release regional revival, the witches and warlocks will be engaging in all kinds of attacks to bind you, weaken you, and weary you in an effort to get you to abort your assignment.

Witches and warlocks also use ley lines to communicate psychic and telepathic information to whomever they desire to communicate with; whether that be with a person, they want to control or with another witch or warlock. This is how we are sometimes hit with psychological warfare. A ley line has been laid in the spirit realm from that witch to us, Break the spell and use the blood of Jesus to dissolve the ley line.

❖ **Demonic Crossroads & Spirits Of The Crossroads**
are when witches work with ruler demons or
demonic agents to lock down an area or territory so
that only demonic activity occurs there. For example,
there may be a section of the highway in your region
where accidents and fatalities always occur. There
may be an intercession or store where something bad
always happens. That is an indication that the spirits
of the crossroads are in operation.

Witches will also use the prince of the power of the
air (ruling principality) over a region to bind the
region to its control. They do this by going to the
center of that community or region and praying a
cross type ley line over the top of the city. They place
an incantation around the city, and they offer
sacrifices to idols throughout the year, as payment for
those demons keeping their crossroads and
incantations secure over that region. As a regional
revivalist, you need to be mindful of this and break its
power, while placing the city under your jurisdiction
as gatekeeper and bind it God and his kingdom.

❖ **Psychological Warfare & Psychic Powers** Witches
and warlocks pray and release spells against
ministers and ministries, especially those that are
called to truly impact the spiritual and economic
climate of a region. They send floods of psychological
warfare to bind, confuse, discombobulate, and clog
the mind, where the person becomes anxious, weary,
insecure, and depressed and eventually question
completing the work of the Lord. Sometimes
territorial spirits and principalities use negative
words and word curses that have been spoken against
ministers and ministries by other people to cause
psychological warfare. These words are lodged on
the frequencies and airways within the spirit realm, as

we must understand that words have life and unless you cancel them, they live in the spirit. The territorial spirits and principalities will open the airways, so you can hear what has been said or they will use psychic powers to direct them at you, so you can hear what is being said and will begin to doubt yourself and question God regarding your destiny and calling. Because some of the voices are familiar to us and some of the voices are even things we have spoken about ourselves, we tend to take them on as our truth. Doing this binds the words to us and gives them power to further bind and discourage our lives.

Learn to discern if the floods of words are coming from your inner man or outside forces and deal with them accordingly. If they are your inner man, then there is some inner healing in your soul, heart, and mind that needs to occur. If they are coming from witches, warlocks, territorial spirits and powers then,

- o Cleanse all negative words that are lingering on frequencies and in the spiritual realm about you.
- o This is your region so command your region to rebuke, reject, and snuff out any negative words ever spoken about you.
- o Repent for any words you have spoken about yourself or others; cleanse them out of the airways as well.
- o Silence any psychic portals that have been opened so that these demonic powers can attack you.
- o Break the powers of word curses, verbally decree blessings, promises, and prophecies God has spoken regarding your destiny, and command them to live on the airways.

- ❖ **<u>Conjuration</u>** is utilizing the dead, demonic spirits, demonic influences, witchcraft, magic, and curses to produce supernatural effects. A lot of this occurs in regions. Especially in regions where there are huge or decent size bodies of waters. A lot of demonic activities occur under the waters, which results in spirits of the dead and other demonic spirits maneuvering in and out of the region. Ask the Holy Spirit to give you revelation of this so you can be enlightened on how to combat these entities and cast them out of your region.

DEMONIC ALTARS & TRADING FLOORS

When we consider altars, especially demonic altars, we tend to think they are built in a specific location and we have to actually go to that location to offer up a sacrifice. However, it is important to realize that altars are movable trading floors and platforms.

Dictionary.com defines *altar* as:
1. an elevated place or structure, as a mound or platform, at which religious rites are performed or on which sacrifices are offered to gods, ancestors, etc.
2. a table or flat-topped block used as the focus for a religious ritual, especially for making sacrifices or offerings to a deity

Wikipedia defines altars (Hebrew: mizbe'ah) "*a place of slaughter or sacrifice.*"

Biblestudytools.com states that particularly in the old testament: *altars were places where the divine and human worlds interacted. Altars were places of exchange, communication, and influence. God responded actively to altar activity.* Altars were a place of worship, sacrifice, atonement, and redemption. The God of the altar governed your life and offered safety, health, wealth, and happiness in exchange for your worship and sacrifice.

In the New Testament Jesus became the ultimate sacrifice, therefore the stationary altar became a moving platform where we can now trade in worship and sacrifice with God through relationship with him.

We therefore, see that platform is not just a constructed area but is any avenue where a person can voice an agenda, expose an agenda, or pursue an agenda for a particular purpose. When these agendas are released, it services as a sacrifice being offered unto the altar of that platform. The purpose or origin of that agenda determines what God is being sacrificed upon that altar. A transaction then occurs between the person and that God to which that altar belongs. Thus, a person trades what they are sacrificing for what that deity is releasing in their life through that agenda.

Even if a person says they serve the true and living God, there no way to agree, sacrifice unto, sow into, an altar that does not serve his kingdom agenda and still contend he or she is not serving an idol God. The person has resorted to strange fire and mixture whether they want to admit it or not. God does not receive strange fire no matter how much we contend our sacrifice is to him.

There are trading floors in the:

> Heavenlies or Atmospheric Realms
> Natural realm
> Underworld
> Under the waters

We have discussed the trading floors in the heavenlies and in the underworld that are governed by principalities and powers and ungodly people throughout this book.

There are trading floors in the natural realm right among us that we must open our eyes to. Some of the little unassuming shops and restaurants are some of the biggest trading floors for witchcraft and idolatry. Especially psychic readings businesses, yoga studios, tattoo parlors, night clubs, sex shops, culture and ethnic focused shops, herbal shops, restaurants with Buddhist and other idolatrous themes. Major witchcraft is being released into the region, as sacrifices and trading services are occurring by people unto idol gods.

TV, commercials, social media, the internet, ad displays at stores, clothing, your job, etc., are all trading floor platforms. They are all altars designed to get our attention and get us to buy into and trade our time, money, morals, beliefs, destiny, life, heritage, etc. for their product. Sadly, because these platforms are self-serving altars or demonic altars, if we are not careful, we can open gateways for idolatry, pornography, perversion, and the Anti-Christ agenda to constantly seep into our lives. Depending on what we take in and give ourselves to, we resort to sacrificing unto idol gods and trading the hedge of God for demonic attacks and influences of the enemy.

Moreover, if we have platforms in these arenas, we must make sure our platform is rooted in God, such that what we promote and release, glorifies and offers up sacrifices unto him. For example, your Facebook page is a platform. What you like, comment on, share, write, and allow on your page, determines what God you are sacrificing unto at the time. Because there is so much being released on Facebook, many tend to have a lot of mixture and be desensitized to many videos, statuses, pictures, etc. that do not glorify God. We must be careful that our likes, shares, and comments have not given way to trading on altars that are not of God. It is also important to be careful that we do not yield our page to idolatry, pornography, and perversion.

We do not realize it, but when we are watching things on TV or listening to vile music that is rooted in perversion and idolatry, we are sacrificing our purity, dream realm, sleep realm, unto idolatry. Such platforms are designed to confuse and desensitize us to sin and wickedness. This gives demons the avenue to fill us with lustful thoughts and desires, sexually molest and rape us as we sleep and dream realms, elude us to compromising the word of God and make light of issues that hold us in bondage. A trade is occurring on the altar whether we like it or not, whether we acknowledge it or not, whether we agree to it or not. It is a platform therefore, it is an altar where transactions are being done between you and that agenda.

Examples of trading in the bible:

> Adam and Eve traded eternal life for the knowledge of good and evil (***Genesis 3:6).***

> Esau traded his birthright, inheritance, and destiny, for food (***Genesis 25:29-34).***

> Jezebel, an idolatrous descendent, usurped the authority of her husband and God to gain control over her region and the people (***1Kings, 2Kings, Revelations 20:20***).

> Athaliah traded the life and lineage of her grandkids by killing them so she could be heir to the throne (***2Kings 11).***

> Sampson traded his purity and the secret of his strength for sex and the heart of a woman (***Judges 16:6).***

> Judas traded his apostolic calling and relationship with Jesus for money (***Matthew 26:27***).

> Leviathan, the king of pride, is a trading floor that operates under the waters. He also operates in the airway through communication and self-exaltation. People willingly and ignorantly trade on these floors for self-glory, to control the airway, communication systems, and patterns. Leviathan is a huge trading floor among social media sites and the World Wide Web. It is also huge among people who want to be

ruling leaders in their spheres of influence. (*Psalms 74:14, Psalms 104:26, Job 3:8, Job 41, Isaiah 27:10*).

➤ A Lukewarm gospel is a trading floor. We are trading at idolatrous altars when we preach the word in error or make light of sin and iniquity (*Ezekiel 3:18-20, Ezekiel 33:6-9, 2Timothy 2:3-5, James 1:22, Revelations 3:15-17*).

➤ When we trade God's will, standards, and laws, for the world's ways or for our own knowledge, we are trading on demonic floors (*Proverbs 3:7, Proverbs 4:19-21, Romans 12:2, James 3:15-17*).

➤ Murder is a trading floor in and of itself. We see this with stories of Cain and Abel, John the Baptist, Jesus, Stephen and other apostles killed for the gospel (*Genesis 4, Deuteronomy 23:43, Psalms 79:10, Luke 23:26-42, Mark 6:14-29, Acts 7:54-60, Revelations 6:9-11*) These deaths are of people with great calls on their lives. Or theses murders can be senseless as witches and warlocks will release prayers for senseless murders as a way of offering up sacrifices to idols. We are experiencing this a lot of regions with high crime rates. The blood of the innocent crying from the land as they are sacrifices to idols for whatever reason. A lot of ancient spirits from tribal times are resurfacing in regions and are the root of gang, culture, and turf wars. Such crimes are senseless murders being used as sacrifices offered to idols.

➤ Abortion is a murderous trading floor. The bible speaks about not allowing children to pass through

144

the fire. We think that because it is a law abiding clinic. But that clinic is a demonic altar where kids traded and sacrificed to idols of Molech, Ammon, etc. (*Leviticus 18:21, Deuteronomy 18:10, Deuteronomy 12:31, 2Kings 6:2-3, 2Kings 17:16-17, 2Kings 23:10, 2Chronicles 33:6, Psalms 106, 37-38, Jeremiah 7:30-31, Ezekiel 23:27-29*).

➤ Israel traded and worshipped Sidon gods – Baal, Ashtaroth, Moab, gods of Syria, gods of the Ammonites, and the gods of the Philistines on the trading floor sea ports of Tyre and Sidon (*Judges 1:31, Judges 10:6-10, 1Kings 16:31, Isaiah 23, Jeremiah 25, Ezekiel 26-28, Amos 1:9-10, Zechariah 9:1-4*). Jesus teaches about how Tyre and Sidon would have been saved long ago, had the saints dealt with the high places and trading floors (*Matthew 15-21-28, Luke 10:13-14, Mark3:7-8*).

Many regions with large bodies of water have underground trading floors in their waters. People who desire high level platforms within government, entertainment, notorious drug lords, gang members, mafia members, etc., willing seek mediums and offer sacrifices to these trading floors, in exchange for power, finances, prestige, and success. People within the region who are under the bondages of principalities and territorial spirits in the underworld, willingly and ignorantly offer up sacrifices to these demonic trading floors.

As we pursue regional revival, we must be careful with where we personally trade, the ministry trade, the saints trade, and those the within the region are trading, as it relates to altars. We must watch where we are trading because we are buying into more than just entertainment or a nice product. We could be trading with an idol god who eventually is going to want more than what the trade was worth. We could be trading to an idolatrous trading floor and further strengthening the powers of darkness against our revival awakening. As revivalists, we cannot ignore these trading floors and think revival will be sustained in a region. It is important to seek God in discerning trading floors in the spiritual realms in and around our region and to ask for revelation regarding the major principalities that rule them. Through warfare, intercession, a drawing the people into repentance, cleansing of the land and atmosphere, planting godly businesses, services, etc., within the region, these principalities and powers can be displaced, and their trading floors shut down while establishing the kingdom of God in the region.

OFFENSIVELY TOWERING IN WARFARE

Dictionary.com defines *offensive* as:

1. making attack, aggressive, of relating to, or designed for attack
2. to be irritating or annoying, angering
3. giving painful or unpleasant sensations: nauseous, obnoxious, causing displeasure or resentment, disrespectful, insulting; displeasing
4. the position or attitude of aggression or attack
5. an aggressive movement or attack
6. attempting to score or one up your opponent

Synonyms of offensive:

abhorrent	embarrassing	irritating	shocking
abusive	evil	repellent	stinking
detestable	hideous	reprehensible	terrible
discourteous	obnoxious	repulsive	uncivil
dreadful	offending	revolting	unmannerly

On the defensive, you are trying to stop an opponent from there attack. On the offensive, you are striving to attack your opponent while gaining leverage or victory before being attacked. On offensive, you are not nice and passive. You are abusive, detestable, obnoxious, and offending to your enemy. You offend demons and witches. They are not your friends or friends of God. They are enemies, and you should treat them as such.

> *Matthew 11:12 And from the days of John the Baptist until now the kingdom of heaven suffereth violence, and the violent take it by force.*

Violent means to *seize, pluck, pull, snatch out or away, claim by force.*" Revivalists and revival ministries ought to be violent and offensive if they are going to overthrow demonic forces and ignite revival fire in the region.

Combating Territorial Warfare & Witchcraft

A skilled warrior learns about and studies their opponent. The warrior is studying his opponent, not because of fear, but to be offensive in warfare. Also, the more the warrior knows and can discern regarding demonic forces, the easier it is to resist and combat them in one's personal life and ministry.

Many would say this is not biblical, but much of the Old Testament stories of war reveal key principles to successfully learning and annihilating the enemy. We are no longer fighting to obtain but from a position of governing over our victory. We must not be ignorant of the devices of demons and wickedness.

> *1Peter 5:8 Be sober, be vigilant; because your adversary the devil, as a roaring lion, walketh about, seeking whom he may devour:*

Sober means to be *"self-controlled, prudent, wise, temperate, governed, and alert."*

Vigilant means to *"take watch, watch keenly to detect danger, be cautious, take heed, give strict attention to."*

These attributes require action, strategy, and discipline.
- Your life should be postured in the appropriate character of God.
- You should be disciplined in your character and faith stance.
- You also should be keen in being able to identify, resist, and destroy the devil as he attacks.

Now the devil is roaming, treading, and seeking. He is on the prowl – on the hunt. He is doing the work to learn you and your life's vision. You must, therefore, do the work vigilantly to learn him. When you take watch, you are on guard. You have already spied out the land and the enemy, so you can implement a strategy to best identify the enemy should he come, and to guard and protect everything from being overtaken when he attacks. It is not a passive position, but an aggressive, active duty of combat.

As the revival warrior studies their opponent, they are learning the following:

- Their character, nature, and personality
- Abilities and capabilities
- Likes and dislikes
- Habits and patterns
- Strengths and weaknesses
- Movements and operations
- Environments and habitats to which they maneuver and dwell
- Their identity, purpose, and mission
- Their personal, geographical, and generational power and operation
- History, culture, language and communication strategies

Spiritual Mapping

In studying your opponent, the warring revivalist is conducting a spiritual mapping of the people, climate, government, and territory, to which they live and are called to. I also suggest conducting a spiritual mapping over regions to which you are called to minister in. When completing a spiritual mapping, you are:

- Seeking Holy Spirit for knowledge of the main principalities, powers, idolatries, witchcraft, worldliness, and perversions that reign in that region.
- You can also drive around the region and receive this information via Holy Spirit.
- Acquire information from online geographical and historical studies of the region.

This information needs to be typed out and prayed into and used as the Holy Spirit leads. I suggest providing a copy to your prayer and support team, so they can use it when warring and interceding for you, the revival ministry and region in general.

In my ministry, we have placed the principalities and strongholds that God revealed to us concerning our region in our ministry's new member's handbook. We deem it important for people to know what they are dealing with. Many tend to leave a region they are called to before it is time because they dread the warfare. If they were provided revelation of what to expect from the demonic realm and how to combat it, they are more apt to embrace their assignment with confidence and peace in knowing they can successfully complete the work God has granted to their hands.

Spiritual mapping allows the revival warrior to be offensive in fortifying themselves against the assignments of the enemy. It is also effective in the Holy Spirit leading the apostle in what strongholds and forces to deal with for that particular prayer assignment. It is not wise to take on every principality and power. Revivalists are more effective in warfare when they operate as the spirit leads. Sometimes, displacing or annihilating certain strongholds can dismantle other ones by default. The Lord will give you specific strategy. It is important to be obedient to what he says, as being obedient and Holy Spirit lead will prevent unnecessary warfare and labor. I decree we are SHIFTING as revival warriors in being sober and vigilant soldiers that dismantle and devour the works of the enemy. **SHIFT!**

THWARTING ATTACKS AGAINST REVIVALIST

It is important in being offensive to know that demons and witchcraft will attack you and to have some awareness of how this may operate. This is just a cheat sheet list of some of the demons and witchcraft experiences you may have as a revivalist. Remember you are **VICTORIOUS! SHIFT!**

- *Zapping Spirit* – Bombards, jolts, snatches, strikes, deletes, steals, kills, revelation, thoughts, and understanding from the mind, such that the brain cannot release the correct information to the people or maintain the information God downloads to them.

  John 10:10 The thief cometh not, but for to steal, and to kill, and to destroy: I am come that they might have life, and that they might have it more abundantly.

- *Blocking Spirits* - Use walls, barriers or troops of demons that have locked themselves together in the spirit realm, where you will have difficulty getting pass a particular barrier. This will feel like a wall, gate, ceiling, door, object hindering breakthrough or a pathway from opening. You may also feel this in your mind and heart where you cannot seem to SHIFT pass a certain thought, issue, or barrier that has lodged itself in these areas.

  Psalms 18:29 For by thee I have run through a troop; and by my God have I leaped over a wall.

  This scripture lets us know that we must run through these barriers. When encountering them, verbally declare out blasting through any troops that have set up siege against you and then use your authority in God to leap over demonic structures.

152

- *Tracking Spirits, Demonic Watchers, Squatters &*
  Hitchhiker Spirits

  o *Tracking Spirits* are demonic agents who are
    assigned to gather intel on you and then report it
    back to their demonic camp. They track you by
    whatever means necessary. They will track you
    from place to place as you move about everyday
    life, through computer systems and other
    computerized intel, etc. They will even track you
    to church and ministry events. They lurk around
    – ease dropping on your prayers and
    conversations, to acquire information about you
    then report back so that demonic assignments can
    be released against you. Sometimes you can feel
    these spirits following you. You know those times
    it feels like something is following you. It is
    probably a tracker. They tend to live on the
    airways, so they rarely will use a body. Although
    they will oppress people in your inner circle and
    track you that way. Or they will follow people in
    your inner circle and track you. Psychics, high
    priests work with these spirits to track clients and
    gather intel, so they can have information to share
    when the person comes for their session. It
    appears as if the psychic possess information that
    only someone in your private life could have
    known. They do because the demon tracked you.

  o *Demonic Watchers* are spirits that are sent to spy
    on you after the tracker spirit has shared
    information on you with his demonic camp.
    Watchers report on your progress so that further
    demonic assignments can be released against you.
    Watcher spirits will even travel to different places

as you travel or send messages to other regions that you are coming, share the intel regarding you, so that the demons in that region can be aware of what you will be doing, and can find a way to counterattack your productivity and progress. Especially if you are trying to save souls for Jesus. In the past, I use to see these spirits traveling by the airplane when I am going out of town to do ministry. I have learned to pray to cancel their assignments, so they do not track me. Many people share all kinds of personal information on your social media pages. Watcher spirits are sharing that information with the demonic camp. The enemy knew where and how to attack the person at because it is on their Facebook page.

In the spirit realm, the devil has a demonic library where he keeps files, especially of people who have great callings on their lives. I have seen these libraries and some of these files. Also, the systems of this world, ignorantly help these spirits to collect and maintain information on us. We are constantly being asked for our updated email address, cellphone numbers, etc., when we go in stores or when conducting business transactions.

It is good to pray against tracker and watcher spirits consistently, as your assignment as a revivalist will alarm to demons wage war against you. Blind these spirits and declare amnesia of any intel they have collected on you. Send them wandering in dessert land until Jesus return or send them back to their camps confused and discombobulated. Declare their kingdom will attack them for not having any information to report. Use the fire of God to zap and burn out any information the enemy has stored on you in his demonic library and computer systems. Cancel their assignments in the spirit realm and annihilate anyway they are working with principalities and powers in my region and other regions to track and attack you. Ask God to place a hedge around you and to give you a stealth bomber anointing, so you can go about undetected to the enemy.

Stealth Bomber Anointing - *Psalms 18:28-29*
For thou wilt light my candle: the Lord my God will enlighten my darkness. For by thee I have run through a troop; and by my God have I leaped over a wall.

Enemies Destroying One another –
2Chronicles 20:21-22 When he had consulted with the people, he appointed those who sang to the LORD and those who praised Him in holy attire, as they went out before the army and said, "Give thanks to the LORD, for His lovingkindness is everlasting." When they began singing and praising, the LORD set ambushes against the sons of Ammon, Moab and Mount Seir, who had come against Judah; so they were routed. For the sons of Ammon and Moab rose up against the inhabitants of Mount Seir destroying them completely; and when they had finished with the inhabitants of Seir, they helped to destroy one another.

○ ***Squatter Spirits*** are short plump looking demons that squat on your property or land to keep the gateways open for tracking and watcher spirits to track you and for other spirits to attack you. Squatter spirits are usually unlawful. They may not have any legal right to be on your land or property. They usually take advantage of you not paying spiritual attention, or if God has promised you a land or building and you do not lay claim to it, they take up residence to and occupy it. Their presence becomes a blockage to you acquiring it. They can sit on land and hinder you from acquiring property and buildings that God has promised to you. They will also sit on your land and manifest spirits of gloom, doom, and depression. That is the reason sometimes you may pull up at events, and there is a dark presence on the parking lot or even in the building. Squatter spirits have laid claim to the land. They are there to make people apathetic, sullen, dull, and dead to the move and presence of God.

When there is a blockage in you acquiring land, a building, or things appear dark and gloomy around your land and property, examine if you have squatters. Put these illegal demons off your property and close any portals and gateways that have opened to give access to other demons.

o *Hitchhiker Spirits* are opportunists. They hang out at gas stations, stores, in appliances and different items within stores, etc., and then get in the car with people and go home with them. These spirits also like to hang out at churches and Christian events and then go home with people. Therefore, we cast the devil out of folks, and these hitchhikers look for vulnerable culprits to go home with and oppress.

Some demonic spirits that are cast out in meetings hang outside the church until services are over and go home with folks they oppressed or find other spiritual homes to demonize. This especially occurs at events with mass deliverance and breakthrough. It is beneficial to have intercessors praying during or after the service to further displace these spirits.

- **_Python Spirits_** - Wrap around a person, family, situation, ministry, or region, while using its body to squeeze and restrict them where:

   o They are limited in mobility and progress.
   o There may also be an unexplainable tiredness and lethargic oppression where energy, movement, and progress are slow or thwarted.
   o There will be a weightiness, physical suffocation, over exerted in energy, and sluggardness to being in step with the momentum of God.
   o It causes confusion, discombobulation, double mindedness, and thought racing, from the signal faculties in the brain being restricted, weighty, and crushed.

Isaiah 61:3 To appoint unto them that mourn in Zion, to give unto them beauty for ashes, the oil of joy for mourning, the garment of praise for the spirit of heaviness; that they might be called trees of righteousness, the planting of the Lord, that he might be glorified.

Break the head and tail of the python. Loose holy fire to torment python where it releases its grip while commanding this spirit to uncoil and be cast out of your midst.

- **_Spirit Of Leviathan_** - Interrupts and distorts communication between the speaker and the listener,

157

between God and the person/ministry, and within atmospheres. Its' effort is to sow offense, discord, irritation, anger, misunderstanding, faultfinding, ungodly judging, mistrust, and suspicion. Job speaks of how Leviathan operates in *Job 41:26-32*. This spirit was in operation between him and his friends who were striving to understand why God allowed the enemy to bring havoc upon his life. This spirit also distorted Job's views where he could not receive wise counsel from God during this time of trial with the Lord. This spirit will enter in when the ministry is under heavy warfare, is in the middle of intense ministry or transition, or is on a time schedule. Quick repentance and forgiveness is the easiest way to combat against leviathan. The unity and love of Christ will dismantle and displace this spirit.

Galatians 6:1-3 The Amplified Bible BRETHREN, IF any *person is overtaken in misconduct or sin of any sort, you who are spiritual [who are responsive to and controlled by the Spirit] should set him right and restore and reinstate him, without any sense of superiority and with all gentleness, keeping an attentive eye on yourself, lest you should be tempted also. Bear (endure, carry) one another's burdens and troublesome moral faults, and in this way fulfill and observe perfectly the law of Christ (the Messiah) and complete what is lacking [in your obedience to it].*

Cut the head and the tail off of this spirit, and release fire to burn its fruits and roots, while casting it out of your sphere.

- *Mind Binding & Mind Blinding Spirits* – Witches love to operate through the stronghold of mind control. These spirits bind and blind the thought life, the mind and senses to cause affliction, confusion, unexplainable fear of people or of failure, and anxiety; have trouble paying attention, experience mind wandering and racing thoughts. This spirit tends to operate and look like an octopus or a squid. You may feel pressure or a tormenting headache, feel like something is sticking you in the eyes, ears, temples, forehead, or the back of the head. Things may look black as you strain to see and discern spiritually and naturally. You may become dull of hearing because the ears will feel clogged or like something is lodged in them. It may also feel like something is sitting on your head or wrapped around your head.

This stronghold of mind control may also plague you with vile, perverse, unnecessary, or unimportant thoughts. Or may have you panicking and thinking of something over and over to distract you from what is presently important. Sometimes this spirit will swamp you with constant thoughts of hurts from your past or present life and heart issues that are unresolved. You may find it difficult to pay attention or to press forward in working on present tasks because of these constant plaguing thoughts and feelings of intense pressure.

Proverbs 15:15 The Amplified Bible All the days of the desponding and afflicted are made evil [by anxious thoughts and forebodings (prophecy)], but he who has a glad heart has a continual feast [regardless of circumstances].
Ask the Lord to sever the tentacles of this spirit or use the sword of the spirit to cut them. Break the power of pressure, pain, and torment, and release healing where needed.

- *Spirit Of Void & Darkness* - May be at work when there are no blockages, hindrances, blinding, binding, confusion or discombobulation, yet the atmosphere, eye gates, imagination, and mind is totally black and blank, dark and empty. We see this spirit in operation in *Genesis 1:2* when God was creating the heavens and the earth.

And the earth was without form and void; and darkness was upon the face of the deep. And the Spirit of God moved upon the face of the waters.

This spirit wants you to think that everything is dead and without form, you cannot see or discern properly, or that there is no potential for creation or manifestation. It operates as a black blanket or cloud, covering everything so you cannot see behind the scenes. It will smother blackness and void over the plans and seeds of God, and even conceal demonic plans so you cannot be offensive against the enemy. It will block out the ability to see the vision, receive revelation, understand the purpose for ministry engagements and events, and discern the plots and plans of the enemy.

Daniel 2:22 He reveals the deep and secret things; He knows what is in the darkness, and the light dwells with Him.

When this spirit attacks, release and declare the light, wisdom, profound, searchable, secretive, mysteries of God to come forth to dispel the darkness.

- *Spirits Of Fear* – Different types of fear can be sent through witchcraft and territorial attacks. Fear is a distressing emotion, concern or anxiety aroused by impending danger, evil, pain, sweating, rejection, etc., whether the threat is real or imagined. It is the feeling or condition of being afraid, frightened, panicked, anxious disheveled, frenzied, overwhelmed, gripped, shocked or traumatized with terror. Fear can be sent as a spell or assignment through the atmosphere, imparted into the mind or imagination through mind manipulation, bewitchment, or telepathy; imparted via dreams, or through demonic creativity or stirring via witchcraft of a traumatic or startling event to incite fear. Fear tends to attack unaware; it can have no real basis for manifesting, but its presence if very real, intentional, and demonic.

2Timothy 1:7 *For God hath not given us the spirit of fear; but of power, and of love, and of a sound mind.*

When we yield to fear, we SHIFT from under the authority, love, and stability of God. We believe the lies, misperceptions, misconceptions of the enemy, while, relenting to instability, weakness, and helplessness. We also resort to believing we are worthless, under-appreciated, devalued, and that our life is not worth living. The more you meditate and yield to the thoughts, the greater the fear and the oppression of its assignment. Fear is an attack and assignment against the truth of your identity and against your salvation and refuge in God.

Bind and cast out the spirit of fear. Break the powers of how it is manifesting, fall out of agreement with any ways you agreed with fear, close portals to it operating again, use scriptures to build your identity and fortify yourself in the love and worth of God.

- ***Spirit Of Confusion*** – Causes chaos, disorder, upheaval, forgetfulness, cloudiness, frustration, blankness, and discombobulation. May be unable to distinguish right from wrong, truth from lies, clearness from distinctiveness. Such attacks cause uncertainty of self and others, uncertainty of one's calling, confusion of one's destiny vision; will cause you to question your identity, your team, supports, and God. You will begin to airways as the chaos causes a tossing to and fro between reality and delusion. The enemy wants you to fear failing, fear doing the Lord's work, fear walking in faith, fear man, fear the devil, fear being obedient, and on and on. Anytime you feel fearful, if it is not a reverenced fear from the Lord or God warning you about something, then deal with it as a demonic attack.

1Corinthians 14:33 For God is not the author of confusion, but of peace, as in all churches of the saints.

Break the powers and spells of confusion and bewitchment. Cleanse out all effects of how the spirit is operating in your life, atmosphere, and ministry.

- *Spirit Of Sluggardness* – The spirit of the sluggardness is sent to cause inactivity, idleness, laziness, relaxed, dull, and disinterested. There may be an exhaustion where you are sleeping for long periods of time or for no apparent reason, not wanting to be bothered, or wanting to hide from people and responsibilities. You can be indolent, slow moving, sluggish, averse or disinclined to work, be active, or to exert energy. This spirit will cause you to lack wisdom, vision, and energy in knowing when to plant, work, and invest. It feels like a weight laying upon you. It can sometimes feel cold clammy, wet, moist, or slimy where you feel uncomfortable or unclean. You have an intent and heart to work, but no drive.

Matthew 26:41 Watch and pray, that ye enter not into temptation: the spirit indeed is willing, but the flesh is weak.

Proverbs 6:6-9 Go to the ant, thou sluggard; consider her ways, and be wise: Which having no guide, overseer, or ruler, Provideth her meat in the summer, and gathereth her food in the harvest. How long wilt thou sleep, O sluggard? when wilt thou arise out of thy sleep?

Bind and cast out the spirit of the sluggard. Break its power off your physical body, health, mind, and heart. You may also have to break its power off the body, health, mind, and heart of your ministry, region and people you oversee. Cleanse your foundation, life and ministry of any patterns of sluggardness, laziness, making excuses, and inconsistency.

- ***Spirit Of Slander & Accusation*** – Releasing fiery darts, word curses, accusations, gossip, ungodly reports, malice, and defamation against one's character, ministry, or work. The slander is generally false or the true being used in a slanderous way to incite shame, shunning condemnation, and destruction.

Sometimes you cannot resolve slander in the natural; it often has to be dismantled in the spirit realm. When slander cannot be resolved, know that God judges the slanderous.

Matthew 12:36 *But I tell you that every careless word that people speak, they shall give an accounting for it in the day of judgment.*

Other times slander can be resolved through healthy conflict resolution skills and healthy communication. But the spirit of slander and accusation is still at work in your soul and in the spirit. It will need to be rebuked, and its assignment will need to be cancelled. The true report of the Lord will need to be declared into your life and the spirit realm.

Proverbs 11:9 The Amplified Bible *With his mouth the* *godless man destroys his neighbor, but through knowledge and superior discernment shall the righteous be delivered.*

Proverbs 26:20-22 *Where no wood is, there the fire goeth out: so where there is no talebearer, the strife ceaseth. As coals are to burning coals, and wood to fire; so is a contentious man to kindle strife. The words of a talebearer are as wounds, and they go down into the innermost parts of the belly.*

- ***Spirits Of Affliction & Infirmities*** – Sometimes revivalists will endure constant or seasonal attacks in this area. Some attacks may be related to soul issues or a part of the generation lineage. God may send an affliction as a form of buffeting to keep the revivalist humble and submitted to him. Other times afflictions and infirmities are sent by witches and territorial spirits to bind, distract, hinder, and attack the revivalist. When words curses are released, they may come in the form of affliction. It is important for revivalists to really pray over their food because the enemy and witches will inflict by casting spells upon meals and drinks.

Many times, we may go to the doctor, and they are not able to cure or relieve us of ailments. When there are no open doors for the affliction and infirmities, then it is most likely due to territorial warfare or witchcraft. As a revivalist, it is also possible to carry the afflictions of the people, ministry, land, and region you are governing. Often when I pray deliverance and healing prayers for myself, I pray for these areas as well for when they are delivered and healed, I at times am relieved of afflictions and infirmities.

There are also instances where I will manifest the ailments of the region or the witches and territorial spirits of the region are attacking me because of the

164

calling and mantle upon my life. If the region is afflicted with sickness and disease, you may incur different afflictions as it relates to what is in the region. The Holy Spirit can reveal to you how to counterattack this to judge and break whatever is binding you such that deliverance is your portion.

> *Psalms 34:17-20 The righteous cry, and the Lord heareth and delivereth them out of all their troubles. The Lord is nigh unto them that are of a broken heart; and saveth such as be of a contrite spirit. Many are the afflictions of the righteous: but the Lord delivereth him out of them all. He keepeth all his bones: not one of them is broken.*

God has promised to deliver the righteous from every affliction. This is so key to remaining in a posture of peace and confidence that he will deliver, especially when the affliction and infirmity releases feelings and reports of helplessness, no cure or death. But you know God will deliver you. Trust him and not your feelings or reports of man.

- *__Spirit Of Jezebel__* – Jezebel tends to manifest everywhere (e.g., on the job, in your ministry, on your team, in the service, in the boardroom, at the grocery story, at the family gathering, online, in your email). I believe this spirit tracks revivalists and prophets. It also shape shifts from person to person, where it manifests in different situations in the prophet's and the revivalist's life. Though some people you encounter will have the Jezebel spirit, this spirit also oppresses insecure people or people who have a need to be validated. It uses them to frustrate, control, intimidate and challenge the mantle and work of the revivalist.

Jezebel will seduce, manipulate people and situations to

stir up strife against the revivalist and the work of the revivalist. Jezebel will gain personal knowledge on the revivalist, particularly about their past, then use it to launch witchcraft drama and conflict against the revivalist and the vision of the ministry. This spirit is so manipulative and webbing, that it will have you questioning yourself even though your motives of pure for the people and work at hand, you are delivered from that sin, and you have not done another wrong.

Jezebel must be confronted naturally and spiritually. Its' actions must be exposed in both realms such that the influences and works are totally annihilated off the people, ministry, region; and in regards to any seeds and fruits, it may have planted within the word of people, ministries, and the region. When confronted Jezebel will be defensive, prideful, and will seek to gain the approval and strength of the naysayers to prove that her actions are Godly and for the good of the people and the ministry. Jezebel is intelligent, skilled, and knows how to articulate where its' plot sounds like the true will of the Lord. The situation will most likely get messy and very confrontational, even unto death (spiritually and or naturally), before it gets better. Jezebel, however, will not submit to leadership or the vision of the ministry, as it usurps authority. As this is exposed, people will discern its true intent, such that its plans revealed and thwarted.

Jezebel will come at the revivalist very abrupt, matter of fact, and strong. This is because of the demons operating behind the scenes to strengthen her assignment and the witchcraft that has been sent to fortify its work against the revivalist and the work of the ministry. Jezebel is not stronger than the Lord and is not stronger that the revivalist's or prophet's mantle. Do not allow Jezebel to cower you. Stand up to this spirit, deal with it naturally and in prayer, then watch God get glory through every situation.

2Kings 9:9-11 The Amplified Bible I will make the house of Ahab like the house of Jeroboam son of Nebat and like the house of Baasha son of Ahijah. And the dogs shall eat Jezebel in the portion of Jezreel, and none shall bury her. And he opened the door and fled. [Fulfilled in II Kings 9:33–37.]

Micah 5:12 And I will cut off witchcrafts out of thine hand; and thou shalt have no [more] soothsayers.

Revelation 2:20 Notwithstanding I have a few things against thee, because thou sufferest that woman Jezebel, which calleth herself a prophetess, to teach and to seduce my servants to commit fornication, and to eat things sacrificed unto idols.

- *Spirit Of Goliath* – Goliath seeks to defy the name, plans, and work of the Lord. Goliath will challenge the revivalist and use intimidating tactics to get the revivalist to back down from fulfilling the vision at hand. Witches and territorial spirits will send constant intimidating thoughts to the revivalist through the well of Goliath. The thoughts are so intense, piercing, and continuous that the revivalist will start to feel overwhelmed, burdened, inadequate, angry, and want to give up, hide, or separate themselves from people and the vision. The revivalist will not want to war against Goliath for fear that they will be defeated. There will also be natural confrontations within the revivalist's life that will strengthen and confirm the attacks being sent in the spirit realm. These attacks may come through family members, bosses, etc. It is usually through people who have a level of authority and influence and is being used to cower, isolate, and cause a withdrawing of the

167

revivalist from walking in their mantle and from the vision.

Sometimes the witchcraft attacks coming through Goliath can cause pain, such as migraines, stomach aches, panic attacks or chest pains. An unwarranted fear or intimidated presence maybe accompanied with these attacks. Goliath is big in stature and boastful in puffed up chatter, but the revivalist is greater, and so is the authority of God in the revivalist's life. Do not go back and forth in mindless and puffed up words with Goliath. Revivalists know who they are, so they have nothing to prove to Goliath or anyone else. Use your weapons and authorities to smite him in the forehead. Explore the heart of situations concerning Goliath, then use the word of God to stab him in the heart with the sword of God's word and plans for your life and the vision at hand, then cut off his head to totally solidify his defeat against you and God's vision.

1Samuel 17:48-51 The Amplified Bible When the Philistine came forward to meet David, David ran quickly toward the battle line to meet the Philistine. David put his hand into his bag and took out a stone and slung it, and it struck the Philistine, sinking into his forehead, and he fell on his face to the earth.

So David prevailed over the Philistine with a sling and with a stone, and struck down the Philistine and slew him. But no sword was in David's hand. So he ran and stood over the Philistine, took his sword and drew it out of its sheath, and killed him, and cut off his head with it. When the Philistines saw that their mighty champion was dead, they fled.

- *The Spirit of Saul* is a rebellious, disobedient, witchcraft spirit that does not have the maturity to adequately govern their lives, the people's lives, or the region he has been placed over. In the chapter regarding the identity of a revivalist, I spoke about the importance of only submitting to the voice of the wise hearted, as they have clear vision for the destiny and calling on your life as a revivalist. Saul is the people's choice, so this type of covering is allowed by God but is not ordained by God. It is essential to have the correct covering and affiliate partners, as otherwise you can subject yourself and your life's vision to a Saul Spirit. This spirit recognizes the destiny and calling on your life but is jealous, envious and in competition with it. People who operate as Sauls tend to be very insecure, battle inadequacy, are mentally unstable, and waver between loving who you are and hating you were ever born. Their instability will hinder their ability to adequately lead and support you. As much as they will use you or encourage you to go forth in your gifts and calling, they will also seek to kill you and the vision God has given you. You will want to be loyal to Saul, but Saul does not know or honor loyalty. You will not receive the same honor and dedication that you seek to give. And you will be constantly fighting and maneuvering around Saul, such that you respect who they are in God, yet not allowing their position in your life to take you out. Pursue God ordained covering and partnership. And break ties with anyone who begins to operate in a Saul Spirit in your midst (*1Samuel 18-24*).

- *The Spirit of Amnon* uses familiarity, deception, manipulation, seduction, and a false or erred sense of love to strip the purity and innocence of the leader, the people, and the vision. This spirit is perverted because it appears to have the heart of God and the best interest of people and the vision but is internally anguished by twisted thoughts of lust and ungodliness. Not expecting this spirit to be among us, creates the perfect environment for it to attack and defile us, the innocent, the weak, the vulnerable, and the areas where our ministry, members, and vision is not adequately covered or watched. This spirit will only get worse as perversion is normalized and legalized in society. We must create an environment that sounds the alarm on rape, molestation, sexual sin, perversion, and inordinacy, such that this spirit does not have its way in our sphere (*2Samuel 13*).

- *__Spirit of Absalom__* usurps godly authority by acting on decisions and strategies that were not discussed with the leader or leadership team. Whether there was an injustice, a situation they believe should be rectified or addressed, they will take matters into their own hands, with no regard to how their actions impact the leader, the people, or the vision. When Absaloms have decided in their eyes that the leader is weak, passive, or ill equipped, they will continue to engage in behaviors to usurp the leader's authority and will become enraged with bringing reproach upon the leader's name, destiny, and life's vision. Absalom may have the best resolution, appropriate response or strategy at the time, but Absalom is a heart matter.

  > *Proverbs 21:2 Every way of a man is right in his own eyes: but the LORD pondereth the hearts.*

  > *Luke 16:15 And he said unto them, Ye are they which justify yourselves before men; but God knoweth your*

hearts: for that which is highly esteemed among men is abomination in the sight of God.

We can have the right answer, correct response, the greatest of wisdom, but where is the posture of our heart regarding how to present and utilize that information where it edifies God, his people, and his kingdom? Absaloms operate out of emotions, retaliation, and revenge. They are self-absorbed, immature, temperamental, and brash in their actions even though it appears as if what they are doing is benefiting or seeking justice for God or for others. Absaloms will use underhanded schemes and tactics to draw the people and the vision from under the leaders' shepherding, and into the kingdom they are building for themselves. They deem their leadership grand over all others and will use the needs, desires, weaknesses, and emotions of the people to seduce and manipulate them to come under their control.

Absaloms can come in the form of family members, team members, friends, mentees, and spiritual children, as this spirit has some type of inheritance or covenant to the leader and the vision but does not value relationship or covenant. They only value what they deem right in their own eyes and will sacrifice the leader to prove that their way of leading is righteous and justified. David was passive and wanted to spare Absalom because he was his son. When Absalom is not dealt with, this spirit causes generational consequences upon the life of the leader, the vision and that leader's sphere of influence. You must confront Absalom and teach vision carriers of your mantle and ministry how to identify Absalom.

As once Absaloms plans unfold, everyone can be
affected, and so can the generational inheritance
(*2Samuel 13-19*)

- **_Spirit of Judas_** operates as a demonic scout or infiltrator
  for the purposes of identifying you to your enemies or
  the enemy, so they can kill you and the work God has
  granted to your hands. God may allow Judas to be a part
  of your ministry for a specific purpose of further
  unfolding your destiny and revival authority in him.
  Remember Judas was used to fulfill prophecy of Jesus
  being crucified and annihilating the powers of death by
  raising from the grave with all power – resurrection
  power in his hand. Experiencing the spirit of Judas is
  heart breaking but understanding its greater purpose is
  essential to processing through the painful experience
  and allowing God to exalt you to the next dimensional
  SHIFT of revival glory and authority that is due to your
  life. Often, we are blinded by the Judases in our midst.
  But Jesus knew exactly who Judas was and what role he
  would play in his life. Jesus did not be less to Judas
  because he would betray him. Jesus imparted, loved and
  cultivated Judas' destiny just as he did the other disciples
  and apostles. We too must be discerning of everyone's
  role in our inner circle. We must be clear about their
  strengths, weaknesses, and propensities to sin and
  abilities to hurt us, while still being who God has called
  us to be in their lives, despite what they may or may not
  do to us. Study the story of Jesus and Judas and ask God
  to identify the keys of how to handle Judas experiences.
  If you discern that someone is a Judas, seek God as to
  whether the Judas was allowed by him for a greater
  purpose or is a demonic assignment completely

orchestrated by the enemy. If God allowed it, seek wisdom on how to lay down your life and process through the experience, such that you do not abort the salvation that others will receive from your experience. And so that you will not abort the resurrection SHIFT in power and authority that God has ordained for you as he defies death and hell on your behalf. If it is completely a demonic attack, then displace Judas from your life and realm of influence; and seek God on how to nullify any impact his presence caused you and your ministry. *(Matthew 26-27, Mark 14:18-21, Luke 22-23, John 6:64, John 10:17-18, John 12:21, John 13:21-30)*

- *Spirit Of Death, Hell & The Grave* – There are a host of spirits that operate in this category. They can attack the person, families, ministries, businesses, visions, and regions. Often there will be a dark presence and experience of doom and gloom, extreme heaviness upon the atmosphere, over your life, in your heart, and chest. There can be flooding thoughts of dying and killing yourself, suffocating, wanting to die and be with Jesus even though it is not time to leave the earth. There can be constant near death experiences, impending death, fears of tragedies, feeling something bad will happen, demonic dreams to instill fear of dying; attacks spiritually and physically through the spirit of murder, sabotage, and self- sabotage.

  - *Spirits of Death, Hell, & The Grave* operates as a demonic threefold cord against you. It is a prideful spirit as the bible says hell enlarges itself and is pomp.

    Isaiah 5:14 Therefore hell hath enlarged herself, and opened her mouth without measure: and their glory, and their multitude, and their pomp, and he that rejoiceth, shall descend into it.

When this spirit attacks, it tries to exalt itself against the plans and destiny that God has ordained for your life. It is arrogant and swells itself as if it has governmental rule and authority over your life. *Pomp* is *saon* in the Hebrew and means *"uproar, as a rushing, destruction, horrible, noise, tumultuous, crash."* This threefold cord crashes down on your life and creates all kinds of havoc. It causes a major disturbance, disruption, commotion, and uproar in your life and/or vision. Matters are so turbulent that death feels inevitable. But you must understand that as long as you remain:

- ✓ Clear and confident in your identity
- ✓ Clear in who God is to you
- ✓ In alignment with Jesus
- ✓ In his purpose for your life
- ✓ Grounded in Jesus being the cornerstone of your life and vision

The gates of hell shall NEVER prevail against you.

Matthew 16:15-19 He saith unto them, But whom say ye that I am? And Simon Peter answered and said, Thou art the Christ, the Son of the living God. And Jesus answered and said unto him, Blessed art thou, Simon Barjona: for flesh and blood hath not revealed it unto thee, but my Father which is in heaven. And I say also unto thee, That thou art Peter, and upon this rock I will build my church; and the gates of hell shall not prevail against it. And I will give unto thee the keys of the kingdom of heaven: and whatsoever thou shalt bind on earth shall be bound in heaven: and whatsoever thou shalt loose on earth shall be loosed in heaven.

Much of the turbulence and the noise is to get you to fear, become confused about your identity, and God's word and works in your life so that it can have an open door to unleash the plan that is at the gates of hell. It will roar loud, constantly, and like a riot coming from every which way to attack you. You will have to consistently contend to overthrow it, but you are already victorious against death and hell. Jesus saw to that your own stance solidifies that truth in your life and vision. Command the enlargement of hell to attack and turn in on itself and silence every storm and assignment from hell sent against you.

➤ *Coffin Spirits* work with the demons of death, hell, and the grave. Coffin spirits want to bury you alive or before your time. They want to burry your destiny and vision, so you cannot walk in their purpose. You will literally feel as though you have died, been put in a coffin, buried six feet underground, and covered with dirt. The grave spirit locks you down where you cannot get out of the coffin. Life will appear dark, gloomy, hopeless as if there is no escape, and you will feel like you are suffocating and trapped in a buried coffin. But you have the keys to heaven and earth, to bind and to loose. Rebuke and judge the threefold cord of death, hell, and the grave, break the locks and seal of the coffin spirit and bury every spirit in the coffin that tried to bury you.

➤ *Premature Death* is when a person, vision, business, ministry, etc., dies before its God appointed time. Many believe premature deaths are preventable. There could be some truth to that in some cases. One of the ways the Lord has had me combat premature death in my life is to examine the family illnesses, health challenges, sin and behavioral patterns, and make changes so that these issues will not be a factor in my life. I have also examined this with the Lord concerning my destiny and life's vision. As I have considered the demonic and unhealthy family patterns and how to thwart them, my destiny has prevailed against premature death spirits that do not want me to succeed in life. Regionally, I have examined with the Lord how this spirit operates against ministries, businesses, and those chosen to do a great work for the Lord. I have received some valuable keys from the Lord for pressing, contending, and sustaining against this spirit where I will not succumb to regional death spirits, and how to help others in this area.

➤ *Spirits of Abortion* is when the enemy wants to abort what God has breathed life on. The enemy will always try to get you to quit, give up, throw in the towel, and sabotage your own progress. He will always be sending plans to abort your revival fire, your vision, and to stop the work of the Lord that you are doing. Especially at the beginning of launching your revival vision, this spirit will be on a mission to kill, still, and destroy you and your work. There will be a constant contending you will have to do to fortify yourself against this spirit. As you begin to sustain in your revival vision, the attacks from this spirit will lesson but remain alert and vigilant as it will always be looking for an entryway into your life and vision.

➤ *Stillborn Spirits* is when you give birth to a baby, vision, business, ministry, etc., but it is born dead. It is lifeless without fruit, substance, or the breath of life. Generally stillborn occurs because what you were birthing stopped developing, failed to fully develop, failed to advance in its process or success while in the womb, was hindered in tapping into its actualized potential, or did not realize or was cultivated in its own value or worth, the womb had some complications or infractions, therefore it did not progress and birth forth properly. Sometimes we can become aware of a stillborn in the womb, but often we are not aware of a stillborn until it is born. Either way, the experience is heart wrenching, and whether we have an open door or not, the experience appears as happenstance, it is a demonic attack on what God has granted to your hands, so deal with it accordingly.

➤ *Spirits Of Suicide* floods you with thoughts of hopelessness, worthlessness, rejection, lack of purpose for living or going forward, doom, and gloom. Makes you feel like killing yourself is the only option for coping with whatever you are experiencing in life. This is a demonic coping skill as God would never want you to kill yourself and even to consider it as an option for handling life matters is demonic in nature. This spirit wants you to be responsible for killing your own destiny and life's success. Sometimes there is nothing challenging occurring, and this spirit will attack. Especially if you have entertained this spirit at some point in your life, then it will visit you at times in an effort to get you to agree with taking your own life. This spirit has increased its assault on the world as even children are considering suicide as an option for handling life experiences. We must be aware of the wiles of this spirit and seek to thwart it in our lives, families, and regions.

Many people will encounter these spirits but will not pray against them. It is important to be offensive against these attacks and not take them lightly. Cancel witchcraft spells and assignments, rebuke spirits of death – send them back to hell if necessary. Cleanse out dream impartations of fear, death, and tragedy and cancel assignments sent through dreams. Continually agree and decree out life and that more abundantly over yourself, vision, and ministry partners. Remember as revivalist; you have resurrection power. Use it to overthrow the enemy.

> *John 10:10* *The thief cometh not, but for to steal, and to kill, and to destroy: I am come that they might have life, and that they might have it more abundantly.*

> *James 5:16* *Confess your faults one to another, and pray one for another, that ye may be healed. The effectual fervent prayer of a righteous man availeth much.*

I decree that you would always have a desire to pray, a love to pray, a fervency to pray, and that perseverance in prayer and warfare is infused into your mantle and calling. I decree that you are fearless and fierce against demons and demonic attacks. I decree that every demon that combats you will be quickly exposed, that you take joy in knowing that you prevail over every demon and that the end result is that you are victorious. May you SHIFT with increasing in your identity and authority even now. May you SHIFT in towering all the more in wearing the truth of your mantle, experiencing God, and him receiving limitless glory out of your life and revival vision. **SHIFT!**

OVERTHROWING PRINCIPALITIES & STRONGHOLDS

In this chapter, I will share some principalities that I have encountered during regional work to activate your mantle all the more in identifying, discerning, and mapping the operations of demonic forces. As you study this chapter, ask Holy Spirit to identity the principalities, territorial spirits, powers, etc., in your region so you can journal them and use it to BEAT DEVILS DOWN!

- **LEVIATHAN** - Operates through a curse (curse can be generational or otherwise). It is the king demon of pride that seeks to steal the kingly anointing. Pride operates greatly among traditional, personal, spiritual, and political and family beliefs. Regionally there is can be a haughty disposition among the people and even in the atmosphere of the region. This is a controlling spirit that desires self-glory; the desire to be served, glorified, be known among people. Attacks wealthy ministries and businesses and releases a climate and aroma where they present themselves as better than everyone else. Jezebel gives this demon power through false gifts, healings, miracles, etc., to seduce people from their rightful place in life and the kingdom. Seeks to stop growth in a person or region by having them glorify self rather than God or above God. Also works with schizophrenia and its attachment spirits. This principality attacks in another way in that it can cause of learning disabilities, and will work with the deaf and dumb spirit to disable the learning, or hearing of a person or region. Can be the reason a person cannot speak in tongues. Causes miscommunication where this spirit gets in the middle of conversations and hearing and distorts or mutter what is said so that there is a miscommunication and/or misunderstanding and twisting of words to cause confusion and disorder). Will dig its tail into the person or region and wraps itself around its victim or region suffocating it (Snatch out his tail, crush his head and severe the body). Other spirits that work with this principality are as followed:

- ❖ Serpent Spirit – Sly, craftiness, and conning spirit; can also be a python that constricts, cobra which is a highly venomous (poisonous) spirit, or leviathan spirit. Can wraps itself around neighborhoods, communities, or the region as a whole or slithers over and about the region to release venom, crafty schemes, etc.
- ❖ Religious Spirit, False Doctrine, False Prophecy, and Legalism.
- ❖ Spirit of Traditionalism - Change is not easily initiated or embraced.
- ❖ Sabotage & Self Sabotage - This spirit works with the destiny killing spirit to sabotage progress, destinies, marriages, ministries, businesses. It comes through psychological and mental warfare where it plagues people and regions with demonic and vile voices, so they will quit and want to move out of the region.
- ❖ Racism – Can work within the church, in communities, in the politics and climate of the community and in the region.
- ❖ Lying Tongue, Tale bearing, Gossip, Exaggeration – Demonic operations are due to personal unfulfillment, slandering others, need to feel adequate at the expense of others; stretches the truth, steal God's glory by fantasized and exaggerated stories that have minimal truth to them yet gives and distorted or false impression of a person, community, or region.

180

- ❖ Quarreling – Can operate in families, schools, and neighborhood kids and families; combative spirit that sows discord, faultfinding, slander, and is an accuser of the brethren.
- ❖ Stubbornness – Resistant to change, resistant to the things of God; there can be a physical stiffness in the neck, neck pain, etc., that can be a sign of leviathan as work.
- ❖ Apostasy - Renouncing or abandonment of loyalty or duty; lack of loyalty and honor within the region and people.
- ❖ Intolerance or Condensation - Has challenges progressing in the things of God or taking in a lot of God.
- ❖ Unteachableness – Resistant to being taught; rather remain ignorant than to be taught or admit an unknowing of something. Make excuses for not needing to be taught or wanting to invest in being taught. Causes people and the region to be stifled of growth due to a lack of knowledge, willingness to learn, and progress pass current state.
- ❖ Critical and Condoning Spirits, Negative Attitudes and Mindsets - operate with leviathan to belittle people and the region so hopelessness to changing overrides the vision for change.
- ❖ Spirit of the Antichrist – Anti-Christ, anti-teaching, preaching and establishing Jesus and his kingdom within people and the region.

- **JEZEBEL & AHAB** - Comes against the apostolic and prophetic voice, the vision of revivalists, those carrying the voice and vision of God, and those seeking to bring change in a people, land, or regions; is rooted of witchcraft and rebellion. These principalities rebels against God's word and authority and the things of God. Counterfeits God's authority.

Works through the lust of the flesh, the lust of the eyes and the pride of life. Focus on self-glory and self-gratification, while drawing people to serve them and idol gods. Intelligent, hardworking, success driving, power driven, power hungry, perfectionistic, and domineering. Uses control, manipulation, lust, and seduction to draw in the hearts of people for personal gain. Tends to have unrealistic expectations of others and uses self-pity and manipulative witchcraft words and tactics to win the compassion of others. Can be aggressive, deceitful, overbearing, extremely or underhandedly calculous and evil. Tends to be unrepentant in how their actions affect others but demands repentance of others who may knowingly or unknowingly hurt or challenge them. Very vengeful. Vengeance is sometimes passive aggressive, underhanded, and callous, but dominated by a strong rage to destroy at any cost and with no regard to consequences of their actions. Can appear submissive and supportive, but usually overtly despises authority, and will overthrow authority to control the people, land, and region. Other spirits that work with these principalities are as followed:

- ❖ Bullying, Intimidation, Combating Spirits, Goliath, Spirit of Saul - Prevalent in the school systems and traditional regional businesses, and ministries. Love to attack fivefold ministries and revival movements to kill the glory of God.
- ❖ Overbearing Spirit, Sharp Tempered - Intolerance for anyone who resists its demands.
- ❖ False Confidence, False Authority, Counterfeit Spirits, Pride, False Pride, Insecurity – Works

among those who have been abused, those who have made lots of mistakes, and among those who are confused about or have no vision for their lives. Provides vision that appears to be God's will or a way to personal fame and glory. Will have people idolatrously sacrificing themselves unto the death for personal growth and success.

❖ Whoredom, Sexual Perversion, Seduction, Fornication work with these principalities. These acts are really sacrifices to idols for ritualistic purposes, fame, power, and destruction of purpose and destiny. People do not know that what they are doing is a sacrifice to idols but because these spirits plaque the region, land, or people, the workings of these behaviors automatically become a sacrifice to idol gods.

❖ Adultery, Divorce – Operates through curses to destroy God's order of family and to destroy covenant with God.

❖ Flattery, Sympathetic Witchcraft, Sensuality, False Enthusiasm works with these principalities to seduce and draw the people unto themselves.

❖ False Doctrine, False Prophecy, Spirits of Error, Compromise, works with these principalities to distort and usurp the truth of God.

❖ Angry, Retaliation, Murder, Rebellion works alongside these principalities to control, incite fear, and chastise people those who do not yield to their rule.

❖ Female Dominance, Male Passiveness, Doubting Manhood, Passive Quitter - Pouting when it does not get its way operates with these principalities to usurp God's will for man to be the head of families and the kingdom rule God has set in place where men are the lead. Feministic movements are on the rise to soften and dismantle the strength and Godly stature, authority, and position of the male role in families, communities, and regions.

* Call evil good – Narcissists, restless and has no peace; never satisfied -speaks contrary to the order of God; is adamant, relentless, bloodsucking, and unfearing in its stance.
* Idolatry, Idol Worship, Witchcraft - self-harming, sacrificing of women and children are prevalent among these principalities.
* Greed, Lying, Manipulation - uses position and false power to manipulate others.
* Lust for material things, worship of enterprise, success, profit, promotion, wealth will be the mindset of the people and the region when these principalities are work.
* Confusion, No Unity, Disobedience, and Resentfulness work alongside to keep people and communities at odds. Strong in gang communities and among ethnic driven communities and ministries.
* Sullenness, Depression, can be evident in a people, land, or region while displaying the domination, effects, and characteristics of these of these principalities.
* Workaholics - Gets needs met through work ethic and through the strengths of others.
* Considering God's things trivial; no godly order is in operation, but manmade and demonic control is evident.
* We must also consider the children of Jezebel and Ahab and Sibling Rivalry - will work with the contrary and/or spirit of competition; will work in families and groups of people. The children of Jezebel and Ahab have their spirit, characteristics, and nature.

❖ Ahabs have an inability to designate and delegate authority, leaving things of GOD to wife.

❖ Spirit of Abandonment works with these principalities as they will have people abandoning children, jobs, homes, responsibilities with no regard to how their actions impact others; this is usually done as punishment, retaliation, or to avoid consequences for their actions.

❖ Denial - spirit causes people to deny even what is in front of them; usually, live in a false or self-absorbed reality.

❖ Spirit of Competition, Covetousness, Envy, Jealousy, Self- Seeking, Self-Serving are all workings among these principalities.

❖ Browbeating Spirits work with these principalities - Even in an attempt to build up people, people are verbally torn down first then built up. This is also a stronghold in the churches, school systems, social service agencies, and households. Rather than instilling compassion, this spirit instills fear, shame, and/or guilt in attempt to change behavior.

• **ATHALIAH** - Mother of Jezebel. Comes to steal the priestly anointing which is the royal seed; royal seed does not just include the children of leaders but encompasses all those under the kingly anointing. They are present and future leaders in the kingdom. This principality works with the destiny killing spirit to dethrone those children and youth that God wants to use from birth to be leaders of their generation. This principality desires to rule and lead in place of God's chosen youth. This principality will even use family members to kill and thwart the destiny of these youth. They will abuse, literally kill, spiritually, and mentally

185

kill the child until they cannot be who God has called them to be.

- **BABYLON** - The spirit of the world, of this age. This is a Canaanite goddess idol of fortune and happiness, the supposed consort of Baal and her images. Historically, Nimrod the son of Cush, a descendant of Noah's son Ham, founded the Kingdom of Babel. According to Strong's Concordance, Babel means "confusion, by mixing." There were a group of people in the bible who desired to build a tower from earth to heaven. God confounded, confused them, and scattered them to deter this operation. The city was named Babel (*Genesis 10-11*). Babylon derived from this place as being the city of rebellion against God. In *Revelation 17:5* Babylon is called the great, mother of prostitutes and the earth's abominations. Babylon is its own kingdom set up directly against and in rebellion to the Kingdom of God. In scripture not only did they have their own demonic altars and treasures, but they often defiled God's altars, temples, and treasures, and used them for their own idolatry practices. Babylon wants to rule and reign its own kingdom of the world, as well as defile and overtake God's kingdom. It desires to overtake the people who are of God's kingdom and defile their temple which belongs to God, and persuades Godly people to come under its customs and idolatry. The world serves Babylon. It is a kingdom contrary to God's kingdom and seeks to govern the people, land, and region with its own self focused systems and principles.

Babylon is rooted in pride, idolatry, self-idolatry, sin, murder-ungodly bloodshed, demonic sacrifices, greed, anti-Christ, evil world system, rebellion, drunkenness, sexual sin & immorality, mixture, polytheism, blasphemy, perversion, inordinacy, lust, magic, witchcraft, sorcery, mediums, psychics, false authority, violence, the harlot, fornication-indulge in unlawful lust, practice idolatry, prostituting of the body to the lust of another, and the giving over to unlawful intercourse, due to being given over to idolatry and serving these principalities. It is strongly rooted in the mindset of people, in the land and regions. Even those who serve God, have some Babylon ways and tendencies that need to be rooted out of their mindsets and behaviors. They tend to desire to fame, success, fortune, and lusts of Babylon while claiming to serve and be sold out to God.

- **BELIAL** – Is a very wicked, vile, undermining spirit of destruction. One of its Hebrew translation means *"Ungodless"* and one of its Greek translation is the word *"Satan."* This lying, deceiving demon cause people to draw away from serving God and his kingdom. It may come to people appearing as a dreamer or a prophet of God with signs that appear to be Godly. Then when the people are enthralled, it will implement idolatrous practices as its intention is for people to worship other gods, not the true and living God. It usually misguides people who are not really sold out to God, or who have open doors and propensities to waver in the commandments and standards of God.

> *Deuteronomy 13:1-3 If there arise among you a prophet, or a dreamer of dreams, and giveth thee a sign or a wonder, And the sign or the wonder come to pass, whereof he spake unto thee, saying, Let us go after other gods, which thou hast not known, and let us serve them; Thou shalt not hearken unto the words of that prophet, or that dreamer of dreams: for the Lord your God proveth you, to know whether ye love the Lord your God with all your heart and with all your soul.*

God demands no compromise with Belial. This is a challenge because many people will compromise the commandments standards of the Lord for family members, friends, jobs, personal gain, etc. They will put aside their biblical principles and succumb to pagan, cultural, and ethnic traditions, with not regard to this being idolatry and witchcraft. This has become such a norm until many are lukewarm and unable to discern witchcraft and idolatrous practices. God says we should be putting these people, even loved ones and anything connected to Belial to death. Meaning we should be despising them and turning away from them, and even turning the people who do them, over to their own demise, such that they receive the consequences of their actions.

> **Verse 6-10** *If thy brother, the son of thy mother, or thy son, or thy daughter, or the wife of thy bosom, or thy friend, which is as thine own soul, entice thee secretly, saying, Let us go and serve other gods, which thou hast not known, thou, nor thy fathers; Namely, of the gods of the people which are round about you, nigh unto thee, or far off from thee, from the one end of the earth even unto the other end of the earth; Thou shalt not consent unto him, nor hearken unto him; neither shall thine eye pity him, neither shalt thou spare, neither shalt thou conceal him: But thou shalt surely kill him; thine hand shall be first upon him to put him to death, and afterwards the hand of all the people. And thou shalt stone him with stones, that he die; because he hath sought to thrust thee away from the Lord thy God, which brought thee out of the land of Egypt, from the house of bondage.*

Regions should reject Belial, and revivalists and revival ministries should judge and destroy the works of Belial.

Verse 11-17 And all Israel shall hear, and fear, and shall do no more any such wickedness as this is among you. If thou shalt hear say in one of thy cities, which the Lord thy God hath given thee to dwell there, saying, Certain men, the children of Belial, are gone out from among you, and have withdrawn the inhabitants of their city, saying, Let us go and serve other gods, which ye have not known; Then shalt thou enquire, and make search, and ask diligently; and, behold, if it be truth, and the thing certain, that such abomination is wrought among you; Thou shalt surely smite the inhabitants of that city with the edge of the sword, destroying it utterly, and all that is therein, and the cattle thereof, with the edge of the sword. And thou shalt gather all the spoil of it into the midst of the street thereof, and shalt burn with fire the city, and all the spoil thereof every whit, for the Lord thy God: and it shall be an heap for ever; it shall not be built again. And there shall cleave nought of the cursed thing to thine hand: that the Lord may turn from the fierceness of his anger, and shew thee mercy, and have compassion upon thee, and multiply thee, as he hath sworn unto thy fathers;

Belial causes younger generations who were raised in the church or those who know the way of the church, to turn to perverse ways and bring reproach upon the church.

1Samuel 2:12 Now the sons of Eli were sons of Belial; they knew not the Lord.

Eli was a high priest in Israel, yet his sons did not have relationship with the Lord or have no regard for the ways of the Lord.

Verse 22-25 Now Eli was very old, and heard all that his sons did unto all Israel; and how they lay with the women that assembled at the door of the tabernacle of the congregation. And he said unto them, Why do ye such things? for I hear of

your evil dealings by all this people. Nay, my sons; for it is
no good report that I hear: ye make the Lord's people to
transgress. If one man sin against another, the judge shall
judge him: but if a man sin against the Lord, who shall
intreat for him? Notwithstanding they hearkened not unto
the voice of their father, because the Lord would slay them.

Eli's sons not only sinned, but they also sinned on the
church steps. They defiled the temple and gave the
impression to onlookers that this behavior was okay.
Despite knowing the laws of God, they had no regard for
their life or the consequences of their actions. And even
though Eli verbally confronted them, he did not stop
them from bringing reproach upon the Lord and the
Lord's house.

This is how the spirit of Belial operates. It will have
reputable saints resorting to a respect of persons when it
comes to the ways of the Lord. This is the reason some
people in the church can sleep around and sin and still be
allowed to preach and minister, while others are sat
down and chastised for their actions. This is one of the
reasons the world does not want to come to church and
why many who have been hurt within the church do not
want to return. There is blatant sin done against God in
the open among the saints, by leaders and sheep, but
everyone keeps having church like nothing is wrong with
these behaviors. When onlookers say something about
the reproach, no consequences are ensued. And the
leaders who operate in Belial behaviors will play the "*I*
am human" card, or will make the saints feel like they
have no right to confront their sin. The scripture "*touch*
not my anointed, "has been inappropriately used to avoid
accountability of treacherous behaviors among leaders
(**Psalms 105:15**). Leaders are held to a higher standard,
and there is no way around that (**Provers 16:12, Matthew**

18:6, Acts 20:18, James 3:1, Hebrews 13:17). This was one of the reasons Eli was judged. He was held accountable for not implementing the same consequences for his sons that he would have for anyone else who had done such file things on the doorsteps of the Lord.

> *2Chronicles 6:16-18 Now therefore, O LORD God of Israel, keep with thy servant David my father that which thou hast promised him, saying, There shall not fail thee a man in my sight to sit upon the throne of Israel; yet so that thy children take heed to their way to walk in my law, as thou hast walked before me. Now then, O LORD God of Israel, let thy word be verified, which thou hast spoken unto thy servant David. But will God in very deed dwell with men on the earth? behold, heaven and the heaven of heavens cannot contain thee; how much less this house which I have built.*

I believe the Spirit of Belial uses the offenses of church hurt and the falls of Christian leaders to cause saints to rebel against coming to church and to be suspicious of being connected to, sowing into, and fellowshipping with the church. The other challenge is that this spirit has caused the body of Christ to be a church divided against itself. I say this because even though leaders and ministries recognize that church hurt has occurred, many of them have not made changes within themselves, their ministry teams, the relationship dynamics and ministry climates of the ministries, where people will feel safety to be restored to the church. We, therefore, have one side bashing the church and the other side demanding that rebels return to the church. Those that are bound to church hurt and has rejected the church are now experiencing some misalignment with their destiny and calling, which is the plan of the spirit of Belial. He wants to destroy God ordained destinies. These people attempt to reorder their destiny by serving God at home, doing ministry on social media sites, etc., while their church hurt spills onto others that they minister to. The leaders and ministries that are demanding the hurt to return tend to operate in pride, entitlement, a lack of compassion and regard for the trauma they have endured at the hands of leaders and saints within the church. They do not realize that if they do not transform their hearts towards those hurt by the church, it impacts them and the body of Christ, as there is no salvation or ministry if people do not want to be a part of it. People need to be aware of how this spirit is operating because it is wreaking havoc in the body of Christ.

- **BAAL** – Baal means Lord. Historically, Baal is an ancient idolatrous Canaanite god worshipped within regions. He was the supreme god worshiped in Canaan and Phoenicia. He is known as a fertility god who enables the earth to produce crops and helps people to produce children. Those who worship him believe that Baal he is in absolute control over nature and over people. They believe he has charge over the rain and the weather, and man's survival was dependent upon this god's provision. Different regions worshipped Baal in different ways, and special denominations of Baalism are at work in the earth. Regions that rely heavily on agriculture and the weather to produce wealth are strongly rooted in Baal worship. Baal worship also consists of sensuality, and involves ritualistic prostitution in the temples; some of the reasons for human trafficking, prostitution houses, brothels, and strip clubs is due to the oppression of this principalities. Sexual worship, prostitution, human sacrifice of children, ungodly bloodshed, fertility, good fortune, wealth, god of thunder, lightning, winter storms, vegetation, magic, self-mutilation, sexual immorality, incest, god of the sun are a few of its origins. It is important to consider Baal worship where there is a lot of senseless murder in regions. Witches and warlocks are releasing curses and spells to incite killings, so the blood goes into the land and is offered up as a sacrifice to Baal. We just think people have no regard for life and are killing one another. But they are under the domination of principalities and powers that use their godless lifestyle and life hardships as open doors to demonic operations.

Human sacrificing is also a practice of Baal worship, especially the sacrificing of a firstborn child. The priests of Baal also appeal to their god in wild abandon worship that includes loud, ecstatic cries and self-inflicted injury, cutting of another person, or the sacrificing of an animal. In *1Kings 17*, you will find the prophet causing a drought to stifle the workings of Baal. In *1Kings 18*, you can study the prophet showdown between Elijah and the prophets of Baal. Baal prophets love to attend ministry events and challenge the ministers in the spiritual realm. This is the reason you will hear a minister say, "I know a witch is in here." These Baal prophets will be contending and attempting to inflict the minister as they proclaim the gospel. The minister is discerning this behavior and exposing the witch. I saw do more than expose it by acknowledging its presence among you, judge it and kill its workings by speaking God's judgement over it and cancel what it is seeking to do to you and the people.

1Kings 18:40-41 And Elijah said unto them, Take the prophets of Baal; let not one of them escape. And they took them: and Elijah brought them down to the brook Kishon, and slew them there. And Elijah said unto Ahab, Get thee up, eat and drink; for there is a sound of abundance of rain.

Judges 2:12-13 And they forsook the Lord God of their fathers, which brought them out of the land of Egypt, and followed other gods, of the gods of the people that were round about them, and bowed themselves unto them, and provoked the Lord to anger. And they forsook the Lord, and served Baal and Ashtaroth.

- **ASHERAH** – Works with the principality of Babylon as it provides high places and groves that yield sexual acts to demons. The *Asherah Pole* as defined on Wikipedia is a *"sacred tree or pole that stood near Canaanite religious locations to honor the goddess Asherah."* This Asherah Pole is a demonic altar, shrine, and figurine. I know you are wondering the reason I am telling you this. But as a regional revivalist, it is essential to understand your mandate to deal with idolatry. You have to know what the people, land, and region is bond to, so you can use the revival fire to break it off their lives, the land, and the region. I am just awakening your spirit man to greater enlightenment, so you can discern the idols in your region. Some of these idols are ancient and have governed regions for centuries. They are not going to just give the land to you. And they surely will contend with you whether you acknowledge the war or not. You must know that it is yours, break its powers, and gut out its workings.

  Exodus 34:13-17 New International Bible Break down their altars, smash their sacred stones and cut down their Asherah poles. Do not worship any other god, for the Lord, whose name is Jealous, is a jealous God. "Be careful not to make a treaty with those who live in the land; for when they prostitute themselves to their gods and sacrifice to them, they will invite you and you will eat their sacrifices. And when you choose some of their daughters as wives for your sons and those daughters prostitute themselves to their gods, they will lead your sons to do the same. "Do not make any idols.

You may know the goddess Asherah as the Queen of heaven. It is the goddess of motherhood and fertility. Asherah operates through perversion, pornography, sexual immorality, and idolatry. These acts are used to offer up sexual sacrifices to the demonic altar of Asherah. These sexual altars are often found in occult practices, covens, and shrines. We think altars tend to be built in a specific location and you have to actually go to that location to offer up a sacrifice. However, it is important to realize that altars are platforms. Dictionary.com defines altar as, *"an elevated place or structure, as a mound or platform, at which religious rites are performed or on which sacrifices are offered to gods, ancestors, etc."* TV, social media, the internet, ad displays at stores, your job, etc., are all platforms. They are all altars designed to get our attention and get us to buy into and trade our time, money, morals, beliefs, destiny, life, heritage, etc. for their product. Sadly, because these platforms are altars, they have crept into normal society through pornography and perversion released through media via TV shows, music, commercials, social media, ads, and clothing. In relations to the principality of Asherah, these platforms are all shrines and trading floors for offering up sexual sacrifices to the devil – to idolatry. Sexual games are also ways to which the altars of Asherah creep into the lives of youth, adults and even marriages.

Kissing games, sex games, partner swapping, etc., are all trading altars of Asherah. Due to media, it is very difficult to escape pornography and perversion. Even if you are not pursuing it, it is subject to manifest in a TV show, commercial, social media page or while you are searching the web. This has made children more curious, exposed and vulnerable to engaging in sexual acts at an early age while desensitizing the world to perversion and pornography. This principality is strong in the world at large. This spirit works with incubus and succubus (spirits that sexually assault people in their dreams and sleep, rape and molestation, and astral projectors (people who use their soul to travel in the spirit realm illegally). Asherah often uses these platforms as open doors to enter the dream realm to sexually molest people in their sleep. When you watch shows with sexual content or explicit, implied sexual content, you are saying you agree with these acts. Since you are taking in these acts into your life, the spirit feels it has a right to act on that trade. Thus, expecting payment of entering your dream realm and sleep realm and sexually assaulting you. Even if we did not intend to watch something that was sexual, if we are subjected to it, it is important to cleanse any seeds that were sown in the eye gates, imagination, mind, and emotions, repent if necessary, so you can close portals that will allow the altars of Asherah to feel like it can trade with you.

At different times of the year, sexual sacrifices are intensely offered on these altars. As these altars are worshipped by cults, witches and warlocks, an increase of mental and psychological sexual warfare floods the thoughts and minds of people due to the release of these practices into the atmosphere of the region. Such increase in thoughts causes people to give into sexual acts of masturbation, pornography, fornication, infidelity, perverse acts, and inordinate affections and behaviors. Sometimes, it is not the person wanting to sin but being driven to sin by what is in the airways, land, and region. We must be aware of these altars, and how they operate so, we will know how to break people, lands, and regions free.

Deuteronomy 16:21 New International Bible Do not set up any Asherah pole beside the altar you build to the Lord your God.

2Kings 18:4 [Hezekiah] removed the high places, smashed the sacred stones and cut down the Asherah poles. He broke into pieces the bronze snake Moses had made, for up to that time the Israelites had been burning incense to it.

Also, study *Ezekiel 8*

- **PYTHON** - Comes to squeeze the life out of people, families, churches, ministries, relationships, and the region, spiritually, physically, financially, economically, mentally and emotionally, etc. Comes against new ministries, businesses, and visions with a vengeance to thwart and abort the vision and hinder them from planting and developing. Seeks to kill them early by causing constriction and suffocation. This is done through suffocation and constriction. Death is generally slow and painful. The snake:
  - Sits on the person's shoulders and makes them sluggish and lethargic
  - Will wrap around a person, ministry or region in effort to constrict and squeeze out the life, production, zeal, fruit, and success of that person, ministry or region
  - Will wrap around the head, revelation, and vision, and cause headaches, pressure, slow spiritual and natural death.

This principality also works through:
- ❖ Divination/Soothsaying (Gothic, astrology, and Baal).
- ❖ Pharmakia (hallucinate drugs; street drugs, prescribed pain pills, psychiatric drugs).

❖ Apathy – makes a person, atmosphere or region lethargic, sluggish, indifference, passive, cold, lack of drive for life.

❖ Depression – especially strong in the fall leading to the winter months. Winters tend to be very long, the cold weather is bitter and hard, which makes life secluded and difficult. Uses the winter season to steals the momentum of people and vision carriers.

❖ Heaviness (constant feeling of a weighing down).

❖ Word curses and witchcraft spells are released to bring depression and mental instability.

❖ Fear – sluggardness and indifferent feelings and sensations causes anxiety, fear, fear of dying, fear of failing.

❖ Discouragement - hopelessness that tends to hit a person or atmosphere when there are not any challenging situations going on or heightens when challenging situations are present.

❖ Infirmity – will cause sicknesses that comes in the form of feeling pressured or weighed down. Can also cause respiratory illnesses or sensations like the inability to breathe or choking.

• **SCHIZOPHRENIA** – This principality is strong in ministry circles and regions. It makes the people double-minded, insane and weary about life and the things of God. There can even be a weariness in the atmosphere where things are generally chaotic, draining and stressful, even for those who appear to be living the "good life" or a region that appears to be advancing. When things get stressful, often people feel out of their minds. People often use phrases like "*I am losing my mind,*" "*I'm going crazy.*" Schizophrenia also works in the atmosphere, especially churches and businesses. It will make things confused and scattered. Things will not flow, and there will be a weariness, confusion, emptiness and pressure in the atmosphere; even in an atmosphere that appears to be productive, but the seeds will be blowing away rather than sowing and flourishing into that environment. A prime giveaway is when there is an uneasiness, instability or uncertainty in the atmosphere and people cannot figure out what is going on even in what should be routine situations. Also working in this area is the spirit of strong delusion. If given over to Schizophrenia, one can acquire a split personality or the perception of a split personality of rebellion & rejection.

Mental Illnesses, labels placed on kids and the distribution of psychotic medication is a huge regional and even national stronghold. Physicians are quick to label diagnosis and prescribe medication for mental and emotional issues. This is witchcraft and pharmakia at its strongest. Saints are being diagnosed with depression, bipolar disorder, Manic Depression, Schizophrenia and are taking psychiatric medication, and the body of Christ has minimal to no strategy for helping people deal with mental oppression, so they can be set free. Many psychiatric medications can be bought on the street and are easily accessible, even to children. People are taking these medications for recreational use, to further experience Pharmakia altered realities, where they escape the stress, mental oppression, and the challenges of life. Many children are labeled special education and/or with learning disabilities, hyperactive, attention deficit, and are being prescribed medications for behaviors that may be demonic spirits at work.

- **ABORTION** - The Spirit of Molech & The Spirit of Ammon – These are principalities and curses that operate to spiritually and/or physically abort, cause miscarriages, murder, and premature death to the purpose and destiny of people. There are a lot of projects that have started in some regions but are not complete and have been left unfinished for years. A lot of churches began projects, but they fall through or start yet end after a few months or years due to this spirit at work. They will be after your revival fire. They a want you to sacrifice your revival vision to their altar of death. I decree consuming resurrection power to beat this principality down.

- **<u>BARRENNESS & THE SPIRIT OF MISCARRIAGE</u>** – These principalities can operate as a generational curse. Afflicts the spiritual and natural womb, making it difficult for women, ministries, lands, and regions to get pregnant with children and with the things of God. Causes impotence in men where they cannot conceive children or the purpose and plans of God. Works with the spirit of Eve to cause torment during menstrual cycles and cause female problems such as tumors, fibroids, cancer that blocks the womb and makes pregnancy difficult. Makes it difficult for people to conceive, carry, and birth God's vision or sustain in God's vision. Makes the region hard, barren, and infertile where it has difficulty producing the will, purpose, and plan of God. Rages against the finisher anointing as people will start off in the plans, will and destiny of God, but never complete goals or fulfill destiny. The vision miscarried or becomes stagnant and halted. People will carry around visions but never give birth. They remain in the incubation stage of destiny and their life's vision.

> *Isaiah 54:2-3 Enlarge the place of your tent, and let the curtains of your habitations be stretched out; spare not; lengthen your cords and strengthen your stakes, for you will spread abroad to the right hand and to the left; and*

*your offspring will possess the nations and make the
desolate cities to be inhabited.*

The Message Version 1-5 *"Sing, barren woman, who has
never had a baby. Fill the air with song, you who've never
experienced childbirth! You're ending up with far more
children than all those childbearing women." God says so!
"Clear lots of ground for your tents! Make your tents
large. Spread out! Think big! Use plenty of rope, drive the
tent pegs deep. You're going to need lots of elbow room for
your growing family. You're going to take over whole
nations; you're going to resettle abandoned cities. Don't be
afraid––you're not going to be embarrassed. Don't hold
back––you're not going to come up short. You'll forget all
about the humiliations of your youth, and the indignities of
being a widow will fade from memory. For your Maker is
your bridegroom, his name, God –of–the–Angel–Armies!
Your Redeemer is The Holy of Israel, known as God of the
whole earth.*

- **<u>POVERTY</u>** – This principality is not just about money
  but poverty mindset, poor self-perception, poor
  presentation of self, poor housekeeping, poor hygiene,
  poor execution of destiny and the calling that is on a
  person's life. People also tend to be tight wads, stingy
  and make excuses for not sowing and investing, while
  spending money on materialistic and frivolous things
  and endeavors. People are constantly seeking to swindle,
  hustle or acquire a free or cheaper way to pay or obtain
  things. When encouraged to sow into their lives, invest
  in destiny and their future, or to sow into the lives of
  others they are gleaning from; defensive walls erect in
  the spirit around and within them. Many people will
  hold back the little bit they are willing to give with
  minimal to no discernment that the investment is for the
  good of their growth and advancement. This

201

principality assaults churches in an effort to close them down and /or keep them from advancing and impacting the region. As a result, many hustling dealings occur within the administration of churches to keep them afloat. This causes unrepented sin to linger in the churches, which hinder the financial blessings and promises that are due to people and ministries.

Many regions have an area that is severely oppressed with poverty. Crime is very high, and the regard for life is low. This principality works with the spirit of Cain, causing people to kill their brothers and sisters as a result of greed, jealousy, and stinginess. The focus is survival at the expense of neighbors, generations, communities, and the region. Most do not feel safe and feel helpless in breaking the strongholds of poverty and escaping the generational and poverty-stricken cycles of the community. This principality targets intelligent, driven youth and people in the community, often causing catastrophes of hardship, murder, and violence to further incite hopelessness upon families and the community. Destiny killing spirits, spirits of tragedy, and death and hell run rampant in these communities snuffing out royal seeds that have been chosen by God to break the powers of poverty and idolatry while restoring the name and blessings of God back into the generational lineage.

- **SEXUAL PERVERSION** – We seem to be driven in a sex driven age. The desire for purity and the protection of innocence and holiness is a rarity. The need to contour and alter one's looks, body parts, etc., has stolen the identity and divine beauty of many as we strive to appear more sexually and sensually appealing to one another rather than to God. Sex is everywhere, and the crossing of boundary lines and standards has made it difficult not to be violated by the perversions and twisted mindsets and behaviors of others.

- ❖ Homosexuality – Huge stronghold among males, teenagers and college students; teens are becoming comfortable with homosexuality due to abuse, videos, inordinate friendships, experimentation, playing sex games, and rap music. There is an agenda released in the world to normalize homosexuality to distort God's will and standard for marriage and family and stifle the purity of children being born through Godly marriage covenants and family covenants. This agenda is also being used to silence saints and ministries from speaking against sin, proclaiming the gospel of Jesus Christ while releasing reproach and judgmental distain upon the body of Christ so cannot save souls and advance the kingdom of God in the earth.
- ❖ Sexual Abuse, Physical Abuse, Incest, Wounded Spirit, Hate – These are strongholds of secrecy among the generations, within family homes, and ministries. They have become more prevalent to the point of yielding the mindset that it is okay and is a part of family and ministry culture.
- ❖ Incubus, Succubus, Nightmare Spirits – These perverse spirits attack people as they sleep at night. They sexually molest and rape people while they sleep or through their dream realms, or insight terror and fear. They instill demonic impartations and fruit into people to further make them crave for perverse and twisted experiences and have propensities for sin, perversion, blood, ungodliness, etc.
- ❖ Spirits of Bondage, Addictive Spirits - particularly cigarettes, marijuana, alcohol, and sex).
- ❖ Sex Trafficking, Prostitution, Pedophilia have run rampant in regions as these serve as underground

agencies for kidnapping, raping, trading, and selling women and children. Pedophilia has become such an epidemic that pedophiles are seeking to have laws passed where they can marry children.

- **<u>GLUTTONY</u>** - Gluttony is a principality of unfulfillment in a person, land, or region where it can never get enough. The effects of gluttony can be seen physically, but the empty portal to which it operates, and gorges can only be discerned spiritually. This spirit devours whatever it oppresses. You can see the potential of that person, region, or thing, but they are engorged by the overconsumption of this spirit. The identity has been so filled with excess that it steals the usefulness, healthiness, strength, balance, stability, and purpose of that which it oppresses. This is the reason some people, ministries, and regions, appear to have a lot going on – have a lot of activity and opportunity, but are producing no real fruit. They are full of things that taste good but are not Godly or healthy. The world will have you think more is success. There is this need to indulge and obtain without even considering the necessity of that matter or thing. Be careful not to allow this principality to seek into your regional revival vision. Stay God driven, and God focused, where your appetite is to feast on him. Cancel every way this spirit influences the saints and your ministry, where there is constant teaching and equipping, but minimal desire to walk in the things of God. People will gorge and stay fat – dying on the pews. This kills revival fire.

  - ❖ Spirit of the Crab - this spirit grabs hold of people, businesses, regions, refuse to let go. It is a possessive spirit that has no vision and holds others down, so they will not pursue vision. It often works with gluttony and sexual perversion as the gluttony and perversion is lodged in its claws, which makes deliverance from sexual and gluttonous issues difficult. As you contend with glutton and sexual perversion, break the claws of the crab spirit.

- **SPIRIT OF INFIRMITY** - Usually generational, territorial, cultural, and operates through a curse. In this day and age, the world systems are designing ways to make us sick, so they can prosper off us being unwell.
  - ❖ Allergies, arthritis, asthma, bent body, and spine, bleeding, cancer, chronic diseases, colds, diseases, disorders, epilepsy, feebleness, fungus infections, hallucinations, hay fever, heart attack, impotent, infections, insanity, lameness, lingering physical trauma, lingering spirit, madness, mania, mental illness, oppression, paralysis, paranoia, physical disorder, retardation, schizophrenia, senility, sinusitis, spirits of death, torment, virus, bacteria infections, leaky gut, weakness, wounded spirit, diabetes, blood pressure problems, cholesterol problems, tumors and health problems among the male and female reproductive organs.

  - ❖ Due to idolatry and rampant unrepentant sin in America and the world at large, we have an epidemic of malignant diseases and tumors, particularly cancer. Cancer has become an epidemic that is stealing the lives and destinies of people and generations. Cancer has instilled fear in the world such that much of what we eat, clean with, complete daily tasks with, etc., has been marked as an open door to cancer. People have become more health conscious more than ever, yet it has not stopped cancer from wreaking havoc upon the world, as the healthy and the unhealthy have succumbed to cancer. This lets us know that cancer is not just a natural epidemic, but a spiritual matter that must be dealt with accordingly.

Cancer operates as a principality, and it has entered society through rebellion against God and rejection of his will, standards, and laws for our lives. Because we have worshipped the creature, we have created things that are not of God's will and design, and have not adequately governed the land where our environment and earth can be healthy, cancer has come in and wreaked havoc upon the world. Some forms of cancer are manmade to instill sickness for the purposes of feeding mammon (pride, greed, and money) and worldly health care systems (Pharmakia, Nehushtan). Some cancers are a result of things we have created that we deem to be beneficial to us, but really are harmful to our bodies and the earth.

Romans 1:25 *Who changed the truth of God into a lie, and worshipped and served the creature more than the Creator, who is blessed for ever. Amen.*

Numbers 21:9 *And Moses made a serpent of brass, and put it upon a pole, and it came to pass, that if a serpent had bitten any man, when he beheld the serpent of brass, he lived.*

Information from Wikipedia: *In the biblical Book of Numbers, the Nehushtan (or Nohestan) (Hebrew) was a bronze serpent on a pole which God told Moses to erect to protect the Israelites who saw it from dying from the bites of the "fiery serpents" which God had sent to punish them for speaking against God and Moses.*

King _Hezekiah_ later instituted a religious iconoclastic reform and destroyed "the brazen serpent that Moses had made; for unto those days the children of Israel did burn incense to it; and it was called Nehushtan" (**2Kings 18:4**).

Jesus is who we are to look to for healing.

> **John 3:14-15** _Just as those who looked in faith to the serpent in the wilderness were healed, so those who look in faith to the lifted up Son of Man will have eternal life._

It was not the snake on the pole that healed the people, but their belief that God could heal them that caused them to live. This should be our focus and posture today, "that Jesus is our healer."

Cancer is prideful and haughty. It acts as a Goliath that believes it cannot be annihilated. It also spreads like a famine and pestilence that eats up the flesh of the person and their life. It devours until there is no trace of their legacy. It devours:

Finances	Mobility
Progress	Strength
success	relationship
Generational & Spiritual Inheritance	Vision & Promises of God
Identity	Destiny

It is idolatrous and seeks to change people's lives into an image that is far from the image of God in and for their lives. We need to command its haughtiness to fall in the name of Jesus.

Proverbs 16:18 Pride goeth before destruction, and
an haughty spirit before a fall.

<u>*Pride*</u> is <u>*gaon*</u> in the Hebrew and means:
1. arrogance, excellency(-lent), majesty, pomp, pride,
   proud, swelling
2. exaltation, majesty, pride
3. majesty, exaltation, excellence
   A. of nations
   B. of God
   C. of the Jordan
   D. pride, arrogance (bad sense)

We know that many of our nations have become
prideful and haughty. We have taken God out of
most everything and have made his laws and
standards an option rather than the mandate to which
we are to feast on and live by. Many people only
want God if it benefits them. Otherwise, many have
become their own God or taken up the god of the
world in an effort to live by their own prideful will
and desires.

> *2Timothy 3:1-5* This know also, that in the last
> days perilous times shall come. For men shall be
> lovers of their own selves, covetous, boasters, proud,
> blasphemers, disobedient to parents, unthankful,
> unholy, Without natural affection, trucebreakers,
> false accusers, incontinent, fierce, despisers of those
> that are good, Traitors, heady, highminded, lovers of
> pleasures more than lovers of God; Having a form of
> godliness, but denying the power thereof: from such
> turn away.

It is, therefore, wise for those battling cancer and
other malignant diseases to search themselves and

208

their generations for root strongholds of pride and haughtiness. Though not always the case, this can be a factor with cancer and other malignant diseases gaining access in a person's life or generational line. Pride and haughtiness may need to be dealt with so that malignant tumors and diseases can be destroyed in the person's life and generational line. Pride and haughtiness may also be the challenge of the people and region the person is ministering too. God may allow disease to bring those persons to true humility and repentance such that transformation occurs in their lives and the person's sphere of influence.

❖ Allergies are huge in certain regions; could be due to the factories and agriculture environments, or in big cities where a lot of people drive cars and pollute the air with toxins. In some regions, there are more allergies and sinus medications on the shelves than cold medications. The spirit of allergies operates through the stronghold of the spirit of pollution. Moreover, Satan is the prince of the power of the air, so when we do not govern the air, we are subject to his workings. Asthma, respiratory problems, constant colds are caused through pollution that creeps about the earth. Rebuke the prince of the power of the air, especially during allergy season and claim dominion over him and everything that moves and creeps to bring about demonic infestation as we have dominion over all creeping and moving spirits whether in the air, sea or land. The more the presence of the spirit of God glows into a region, the more the air will be like heaven as these infirmities are cleansed out the atmosphere and region. Declare God's glory into the region.

Genesis 1:26-28 And God said, Let us make man in our image, after our likeness: and let them have dominion over the fish of the sea, and over the fowl of the air, and over the cattle, and over all the earth, and over every creeping thing that creepeth upon the earth. So God created man in his own image, in the image of God created he him; male and female created he them. And God blessed them, and God said unto them, Be fruitful, and multiply, and replenish the earth, and subdue it: and have dominion over the fish of the sea, and over the fowl of the air, and over every living thing that moveth upon the earth.

The words *creepeth* and *moveth* are the same word *Ramas*, in the Hebrew and means:
1. to glide swiftly, i.e., to crawl or move with short steps; by analogy to swarm: — creep, move
2. To creep, move lightly, move about, walk on all fours
3. to creep, teem (of all creeping things) to creep of animals)
4. to move lightly, glide about (of water animals) to move about (of all land animals generally)

We must assert dominion over the creepy things that are taking up residence in our region to make the people, land, and atmosphere sick. We must assert authority in this area in order experience more deliverance, healing, miracles, signs, and wonders, and so our greater works can be maintained and sustained.

- **<u>SCORPION</u>** – Though not always the case, this is a territorial spirit that is usually found in the desert.

Though it tends to be an isolated being, it devours other vertebrates and is subject to other forces. Therefore, there are a lot of spirits working in and of its kingdom, such as serpent spirits, python, addler (**Luke 10:19**), the ruler spirit of the Lion (ferocious devouring spirit), and the young lion and dragon (leviathan, behemoth) (**Psalms 91:13**). The scorpion spirits have poisoned lands and atmospheres of many regions with its sting. Its sting can cause a quick death, which is why murder is on the rise, slander is rapid, and is the reason some regions looks so dead and desolate in many areas.

The Scorpion Spirit also causes torment among the people and looses spirits of fear and pain. It will be essential to tear down these high places and drive it out of the city along with its imps. Suck out its poison in the land, people and atmosphere, and decree healing, fruitfulness and prosperity in its place.

- **LEGALISM** – This principality works with the antichrist, stronghold of religion, politics, institutionalism, litigation, and corruption. Restricts free choice; restricts the workings of the Holy Spirit; restricts the favor and prosperity of the saints, restricts jobs and moving upward in companies and branching out into one's own business. Causes segregation of communities, churches, and racists of people. Operates as a strong territorial spirit within ministries and people; causes them to feel like they have ownership of people, ministries, organizations, positions, etc. because they are a part of those people's lives or those institutions. Very possessive and will fight to hold claim to their legalities.

UNLEASHING THE SCOUTS!
KEYS TO DISCERNING
PRINCIPALITIES & POWERS

1Corinthians 12:10 mentions the gift of discernment of spirits. Discernment is the ability to *"yield a judicial estimation, distinguish, judge, dispute or discern between good and evil, particularly demonic forces."* Saints only like to discern other saints for they are always looking for imposters and deceivers among them.

> **1John 4:1** *Beloved, believe not every spirit, but try the spirits whether they are of God: because many false prophets are gone out into the world.*

We must also be discerners of spiritual realms and spiritual wickedness in high places.

> **Ephesians 6:10-13** *Finally, my brethren, be strong in the Lord, and in the power of his might. Put on the whole armour of God, that ye may be able to stand against the wiles of the devil. For we wrestle not against flesh and blood, but against principalities, against powers, against the rulers of the darkness of this world, against spiritual wickedness in high places. Wherefore take unto you the whole armour of God, that ye may be able to withstand in the evil day, and having done all, to stand.*

<u>Wrestle</u> in the Greek is *palē* and means:
1. wrestling (a contest between two in which each endeavors to throw the other, and which is decided when the victor is able to hold his opponent down with his hand upon his neck)
2. the term is transferred to the Christian's struggle with the power of evil

We must understand that our fight is in the heavenlies, with principalities and powers. It is imperative to have the eyes of our understanding enlightened to discern in these realms and to recognize that it is part of our calling to contend and overthrow darkness in these spheres.

> *Ephesians 1:18 The eyes of your understanding being enlightened; that ye may know what is the hope of his calling, and what the riches of the glory of his inheritance in the saints.*

As one who has experienced demonic visitations since childhood, I had no choice but to learn how to discern and to fight principalities and powers. I did not ask for this gift; it was given to me as part of my calling. My experiences of being attacked by demonic spirits and not understanding what was happening to me, surely caused me to dread that I could see and experience realms that most had no clue existed or feared when I shared a glimpse of my experiences or what I discerned. As I embraced this as my calling and was able to overthrow darkness, I learned that if we do not operate in real discernment, especially of principalities and powers, we will not experience the complete victory Jesus provided for us through his burial and resurrection.

Many are hesitant with discerning demonic realms because they fear what God may show them. I will admit that some spiritual realms are beautiful, and some are horrific and nightmarish, especially those overtaken by witchcraft covens and demonic camps. The average saint will not discern to this dimension as you will discern through your spiritual senses, so you will receive knowledge and insight without all the gore.

Hebrews 5:14 *But strong meat belongeth to them that are of full age, even those who by reason of use have their senses exercised to discern both good and evil.*

If you are a seer, a prophet, high level intercessor, or you are called to a greater authority in these realms, you may see the gore at times. Sometimes God will show you the gore to give you more specific keys to the enemy's camp, or to really enlighten you on how serious dealing with these realms really is. Some of the nightmares that believers have are really God revealing insight into the enemy's camp. But because of fear and lack of discernment, we assume every dark dream is from the devil. Though it may be about the devil, it may be the enlightenment you need to SHIFT your life, ministry, or region from under the bondage of the enemy. God is never going to show you anything that he has not given you the authority to handle.

I had to learn and embrace this truth as I am called to be a military scout for the body of Christ. I live in and from the heavenlies and can discern the natural and spiritual realms at the same time. The challenge with the spiritual realms is many of them are empty, or the devil and his kingdom occupies them. Therefore you can say I live in the natural realms and inside the gates and walls of the enemy. I generally have a knowing of the enemy's camp or the witchcraft that is occurring, and many times I discern things in its raw form. As a scout, I am the eyes and ears for the army of the Lord. When intel is needed on the enemy, I maneuver around the enemy's camp or on the battle ground and collect intel. Or I simply just discern what is occurring and wait on the Lord to tell me what to do with what he is showing me. In the Old Testament, scouting was used all the time as a warfare tactic against the enemy. In the New Testament, it was used as a scouting tactic to seize Jesus Christ for the purposes of crucifying him.

Deuteronomy 1:22 Then all of you approached me and said, 'Let us send men before us, that they may search out the land for us, and bring back to us word of the way by which we should go up and the cities which we shall enter.'

Numbers 13:1-2 And the Lord spoke to Moses, saying, "Send men to spy out the land of Canaan, which I am giving to the children of Israel; from each tribe of their fathers you shall send a man, every one a leader among them."

Joshua 7:2 New International Bible Joshua sent some of his men from Jericho to spy out the town of Ai, east of Bethel, near Beth-aven.

Luke 20:20-22 So they watched Him, and sent spies who pretended to be righteous, in order that they might catch Him in some statement, so that they could deliver Him to the rule and the authority of the governor. They questioned Him, saying, "Teacher, we know that You speak and teach correctly, and You are not partial to any, but teach the way of God in truth. "Is it lawful for us to pay taxes to Caesar, or not?"

Galatians 2:4 But it was because of the false brethren secretly brought in, who had sneaked in to spy out our liberty which we have in Christ Jesus, in order to bring us into bondage.

Sometimes I spy out the land, and sometimes I engage the enemy in the field, track, and report their activity, scout out their weaponry, locations, conditions, plans, assignments, etc. and report this information to leaders, ministries, intercessory teams, etc. This information should be used to explore strategies and plans for demolishing demonic kingdoms and covens. However, because many do not understand or receive this level of warfare, the information that myself and other scouts report are often tossed aside, or ministries think they can pray one prayer and resolve the matter. Striving to get leaders and ministries to implement strategies strategically and consistently to overthrow the enemy's camp is the biggest reason we do not reign in the earth. As a body of Christ, we must want the gift of discerning of spirits even as we would prophecy, miracles, healings, or divers of tongues. When we begin to live through these keys, God will reveal strategies to overthrow these principalities and powers. His strategies are given to his friends - those who have his heart and ear - who want to see his will and purpose established in the earth.

> **Matthew 13:11** *He answered and said unto them, because it is given unto you to know the mysteries of the kingdom of heaven, but to them it is not given.*

> **Luke 8:10** *He replied, "The knowledge of the mysteries of the kingdom of God has been given to you, but to others I speak in parables, so that, 'Though seeing, they may not see; though hearing, they may not understand.'*

> **1Corinthians 2:12** *But God has revealed it to us by the Spirit. The Spirit searches all things, even the deep things of God.*

> **Colossians 1:27** *to whom God has chosen to make known among the Gentiles the glorious riches of this mystery, which is Christ in you, the hope of glory.*

The plans God may give you to overthrow darkness may be unconventional. They may not even appear to be comparable to defeating the enemy, but God's ways are not our ways or the enemy's ways. God's weapons and strategies may seem foolish but will confound the wise. Whatever the strategy, implement it and trust him to bring breakthrough on his terms, through his weaponry, and for his glory. If you are obedient, you will see,

- ❖ Love cast out fear
- ❖ Joy become your strength
- ❖ Praise annihilate depression, execute judgment, and vengeance
- ❖ Devils cast out by the finger of God

You get my drift? God will give you strategies

- ❖ For business endeavors, entrepreneur moves, and on and on
- ❖ On how to displace principalities in the region
- ❖ On how to pull down high places and covens

But you must be obedient to what he speaks. You have to see it as intel he is revealing to you - his friend. I am going to provide you with keys to awakening this gift in a greater way upon your life. Commit to exercising it daily such that you begin to see, engage, and scout spiritual realms as easily as you do the natural realm. Get ready to SHIFT into exposing the devil's camp and overthrowing his kingdom for God's glory.

Keys To Embracing Principalities And Powers

- Embrace spiritual realms as part of your calling (*Ephesians 2:6, 1Corinthians 2:14*).

- Possess a desire to see and discern demonic forces (*Hebrews 4:12, Matthew 10:16*).

- Ask God for the eyes of your understanding to be enlightened to discern demonic forces, especially those in your region and sphere of influence (*Ephesians 1:8*).
- Live a life of daily deliverance so you can be alert and combative against demonic infiltration (*Matthew 15:26, Romans 12:2, Psalms 34:19-21*).
- Know and exercise your authority over all demonic strongholds (*Luke 10:19, Hebrews 5:14*).
- Utilize your faith to ascend and live in and from the third heaven, above principalities and powers, so you can contend from your rightful place of authority in God (*Ephesians 2:6*).
- Want and possess your inheritance of lands and spheres within spiritual realms, as we have land and spheres that are due us in the spiritual realm even as we do in the natural (*Ephesians 1:3 Blessed be the God and Father of our Lord Jesus Christ, who hath blessed us with all spiritual blessings in heavenly places in Christ*).
- Have a desire to judge principalities and powers and to see them overthrown (*John 7:24, 1Kings 3:9, 1Thessalonians 5:21*).
- Possess a heart to see God's kingdom reign in the earth (*Matthew 6:10, Matthew 11:12, Luke 11:20*).
- Assess your authority concerning your right to see and discern the schemes of the enemy (*1Peter 5:8*).

GUARDING YOUR ALTAR

As a minister who was over the Altar Workers Ministry in my previous church for seven years, I am always drawn to watch the ministry that occurs at altars when I attend events. Often, I am speaking in fiery tongues as I watch people from the audience come up and lay hands and pray for people when the Spirit of God is high, and the workers are so busy catching people, and laying blankets on people, that they do not realize that the altar has just been infiltrated. Generally, these opportunists:

- ❖ Have no regard for protocol.
- ❖ May have a heart to be used or want to be helpful, and are an open door in that moment.
- ❖ Is a demonized person transferring spirits to people.
- ❖ Is a witch or warlock releasing spells and curses on people and on the meeting.

These opportunists tend to wait until the altar is packed to attack. They love the people that fall on the floor because no one is watching them, other than to cover them up and make sure they do not get stepped on. I was recently at a meeting, and a teenager received prayer. I was standing by her. She fell to the ground during prayer and was covered with a cloth. An opportunist from the audience came up and started dancing and swaying around the teenager while chanting something that others would have assumed was her prayer language. But it was a witchcraft spell. I begin to intercede for the teenager. The opportunist bent down and began rubbing all over the teenager as she was resting with God. I did not want to be out of order myself but watching this was like watching an inordinate violation of proximity. I looked for workers, but they were all engrossed in catching folks. I reach down by the girl and begin to guard her from the opportunist, and broke the witchcraft curses off her. When the teenager got ready to stand up, I helped her up, and I prayed over her again. But even in that, I could have been one of the opportunists as no one said anything to me either.

Sometimes these opportunists blend in with the crowded altar, and while the ministers are laying hands and the focus is on them, they go behind different people and subtly rub on their backs and shoulders. It almost appears as if they are a part of the altar workers team. The person this is happening to assume they are, so they do not stop the opportunist. Yet all kinds of transferences of spirits and witchcraft are occurring. Basically, they are stealing the impartation that the minister is releasing and filling people with demonic manifestations. This is the reason many leave the altar feeling sick, with headaches, lustful, unchanged, and empty when they should be full of God.

As you are planning to launch your revival events, commit to having a dedicated prophetic or intercessor watchmen over your altar, who can properly train people to watch, pray, discern, and intervene with issues like this. It would be good to just assign people to watch for situations of infiltration. It is also beneficial for altar workers to have badges and even similar attire that helps the team stand out from the crowd. It is also great to have watchmen in the audience as well. Ushers are great, but they need to be trained to be watchmen on the wall. It is not enough to greet people, and lead them to a seat. They need to be able to discern demonic and witchcraft infiltration, and there should be protocols in place for handling these situations.
The larger your crowd, the more people you should have guarding the gates. The altar and the sanctuary are gates. Demons and wicked people should not be allowed to run rampant. This will be essential when igniting revival as all

kinds of people are drawn to these meetings. Witches like to attend and have Elijah showdowns in the spirit realm with ministers. Demonized people attend to disrupt meetings or keep the minister tied up with a demon they are not trying to rid themselves of while being drained of their strength, time, and anointing. I know some will read this and say, *"Jesus protecting them."* Many parents assume the same thing when their child goes in a public bathroom only to come out saying someone defiled them. Or a parent sends a child to a friend's home for a visit, and they come home raped. People have free will, and they are becoming bolder and evil in their imaginations and tactics to deceive. We want God's altar to remain pure and safe where people will willingly come to be ignited with revival fire. Do not leave them uncovered. **SHIFT!**

GATHERING LIKE-MINDED BELIEVERS

As I contemplate revival, I have ignited a lot of revival movements throughout seasons of my ministry. Many of them did not last for different reasons. I will list some of them:

- ❖ I birthed revival where I was not the leader. The ministries operated in the revival fire that was ignited for a season. However, when the leadership SHIFTED to another vision, without continuing to cultivate revival, it snuffed out revival.
- ❖ I have birthed revival and jealous and controlling prophets have come along and SHIFTED the ministry to another focus that was not the Lord or that did not include cultivating revival; it killed the revival fire.
- ❖ I birthed revival among a younger generation that I was more of a surrogate mentor or spiritual parent. I was not the main leader, and I was a surrogate ordained by God to provoke, empower and support them in their destiny as this was not cultivated within the ministry. When God SHIFTED me out of the ministry, the revival that was ignited in the younger generation died. I learned that people cannot rely on a person to awaken revival. Revival has to be built on the Holy Spirit within them. When it is built on a person and ministry, and the person or ministry SHIFTS, the fire leaves with them, and revival dies.
- ❖ I have had experiences of birthing revival in the wrong climate or ground, and thus the seeds of revival were sparked, but not ignited into revival

fire. Or a fire was ignited, but because it did not take root in the climate or ground, the fire died.

❖ I have strived to unit and birth revival with saints who contend they want revival. They have a revelation for the need for revival, but differences regarding beliefs about God, the gifts of the spirit, the Holy Spirit and his workings, stifle the true awakening of revival. We had a lot of conversations about revival, and a lot of events in an effort to ignite revival, but the flames waned as fast as they flamed. In these instances, I have noticed that in many ministries among these saints there is evidence of revival, but as a whole, there has not been a unity of the flames to ignite regional revival.

The most ideal scenario would be for all the ministries in the regions to unify and aide in awakening revival. Though I do not doubt that this is possible, I have learned from pioneering my own ministry that everyone is not called to help launch certain visions. It is important to respect the measure of grace upon people's lives. Otherwise, we attempt to make people fill positions and roles that they do not have the grace, ability, or desire to complete. This results in offense because we have unrealistic expectations of them.

Amos 2:3 Can two walk together, except they be agreed?

I have had people leave my ministry because planting and plowing was not their grace. I have had others who did not want to do the work or wanted a ministry that was already established. I had to respect their choice to leave and go where they felt they would be a better fit. Had I tried to encourage them to stay, it would have caused unnecessary drama, confusion, and even caused a rift in our relationship.

223

None of this was necessary because the vision is not personal. It is God's work. My allegiance is not to them, and their allegiance is not to me. Our allegiance should be to God, and then we connect in covenant and unity through him. People should have a heart for the vision he is releasing and must want to please him in bringing it to pass. If they do not have his heart for the vision, they will be a burden and open door rather than a blessing and asset to the ministry.

One of the ways to discern vision carriers is whether they are able to grasp a clear concept of the vision and run with it.

> *Habakkuk 2:2-3 And the LORD answered me, and said, Write the vision, and make it plain upon tables, that he may run that readeth it. For the vision is yet for an appointed time, but at the end it shall speak, and not lie: though it tarry, wait for it; because it will surely come, it will not tarry.*

In this passage of scripture, God said that those who understood the importance of the vision, would read the vision plan, and immediately be able to undergird and work it. They were not worried about when it came to pass, the work that was involved. They were invested in working the vision and trusting God to bring it to pass.

You may want every ministry and saint in the region to participate, but that may not be God's vision. Many assume the more numbers we have, the more effective we can be. Especially with regional revival. We equate revival to huge venues and big crowds. But large venues and big crowds are drawn into the revival fire because of the blaze of a select unified few who have a heart for the awakening of God. It is because of those who read the vision and in their hastening to bring it to pass, they ignited revival fire.

1Corinthians 1:10 *I appeal to you, brothers and sisters, in the name of our Lord Jesus Christ, that all of you agree with one another in what you say and that there be no divisions among you, but that you be perfectly united in mind and thought.*

One of the biggest challenges with focusing more on numbers than the unity of mind and thought is that we end up having opinions, pet peeves, quirks, and religions perceptions override the vision. We then start to implement rules and regulations that stifle the liberty of the Holy Spirit and the exaltation of Jesus. Jesus must be Lord, and the Holy Spirit must have free reign if you are going to awaken revival. Most religious doctrines differ in these two areas which have caused division in the body of Christ. We have to respect that some people are going to believe what they desire and that as they see the revival blaze burning, they will be drawn into the fire. Or they may hold on to their perceptions and choose not to be transformed by the fire. At any rate revivalists and revival, ministries must trust and even be okay that many in the region will benefit from the revival and even unite later with the awakening, yet will initially reject it or will never be a contributor of it.

I remember when God told me my ministry would become its own entity, I assumed certain people would assist me. But many of these people had hang ups about being a part of a small ministry, being a part of a house ministry, and being apart because I was a woman. God told me I had to release offense and forgive them as in the future they would return to be a part of the ministry and I had to accept them. That some of them would even assist with carrying the vision of the ministry in the future. It takes a humble spirit to release, and forgive. It takes and understanding that the vision is not about what we desire – our plans and perceptions, but about God and his purpose for the vision. I released and forgave them, and I am looking forward to them returning and being a part of the great awakening that God will do in the region.

> **Colossians 3:13-14** *Bear with each other and forgive one another if any of you has a grievance against someone. Forgive as the Lord forgave you. And over all these virtues put on love, which binds them all together in perfect unity.*

It is important to respect who God gives his heart to concerning the vision. I have had experiences where I knew I was to assist people and ministries with launching and establishing a work, but because I was not their forte or fit their personal standard of who should be equipped and chosen to work the vision, I was rejected. There have been instances where I have had to war in the spirit and contend for honor, favor, and breakthrough before I could be and do what God was requiring of me regarding a vision. And in some of those experiences, who I was personally was rejected. But because my gifts, anointings, and heart for the vision was evident, I was reluctantly allowed to be a vision carrier. It is sad, however, to be amongst your brothers and sisters in Christ and only be accepted because of your works and not because of who you are. This happened to Jesus, and he was challenged by it, but he still blessed the people and fulfilled the work God granted to his hands.

> **John 6:26** *Jesus answered them and said, Verily, verily, I say unto you, Ye seek me, not because ye saw the miracles, but because ye did eat of the loaves, and were filled.*

> **John 10:37-39** *If I am not doing the works of My Father, then do not believe Me. But if I am doing them, even though you do not believe Me, believe the works themselves, so that you may know and understand that the*

Father is in Me, and I in the Father." At this, they tried
again to seize Him, but He escaped their grasp.
John 14:11-13 Believe Me that I am in the Father and the
Father is in Me – or at least believe because of the works
themselves. Truly, truly, I tell you, whoever believes in Me
will also do the works that I am doing. He will do even
greater things than these, because I am going to the Father.
And I will do whatever you ask in My name, so that the
Father may be glorified in the Son.

As much as Jesus freely gave of himself, many people did
not receive the fullness of what he invested because of a
select few that lacked belief in who he was. This is what
happens when you receive someone for their works but not
their identity. Despite them giving their all, you only receive
a measure of what they impart into your life and the vision.
Measure means the full operation of the Holy Spirit was not
manifested. Without the liberation of the Holy Spirit, revival
is not completely ignited.

Philippians 2:1-3 If there be therefore any consolation in
Christ, if any comfort of love, if any fellowship of the Spirit,
if any bowels and mercies. Fulfil ye my joy, that ye be
likeminded, having the same love, being of one accord, of
one mind. Let nothing be done through strife or vainglory;
but in lowliness of mind let each esteem other better than
themselves.

God has a team waiting for the revival vision that he has
granted to your hands. The fire is already blazing in them.
They are just waiting for it to be made clear, so they can run
with it. Go forth with the team God has given you and trust
that as you lift him up, it will draw ALL those in the region
and beyond unto him. You God this. **SHIFT!**

TRAINING & EQUIPPING FOR APOSTOLIC RELEASE

As your team members are revealed, they may be from different ministries within the region along with those from your ministry. God may have you connect with revivalists or fivefold ministers/ministries from outside of the region to come help you ignite revival. It will be important to train and equip your team to sustain in carrying the revival vision. Training and equipping is vital to revival as revival is not just about services; it is also about the reformation of the region. If your team is not trained and equipped in their destiny and calling, and have a clear understanding of how that impacts the region, then they cannot impart that into those that will unify with the revival awakening. They must know who they are and producing their life's vision in the earth so that as you all ignite revival, it can spread into the region. In addition to the training suggestions already mentioned in this book, your team needs to be trained in:

- ❖ Personal Destinies & Callings
- ❖ Healthy Family & Social Dynamics
- ❖ Social Skills Building
  - ➢ Relationship Skills
  - ➢ Communication Skills
  - ➢ Conflict Resolution Skills
  - ➢ Coping Skills
  - ➢ Anger Management
  - ➢ Social Skills
  - ➢ Interpersonal Skills
- ❖ Entrepreneurship, Pioneering & Trailblazing
  - ➢ Pioneering Christian Schools, Universities
  - ➢ Pioneering Stores, Hotels, Banks
  - ➢ Rehabbing & Flipping Homes, Buildings

- ➢ Pioneering Counseling Centers, Social Service Agencies
- ❖ Marketplace Ministry
- ❖ Business
- ❖ Financial Planning & Investment
- ❖ Evangelism
- ❖ Real-estate
- ❖ Government
- ❖ Media
- ❖ Entertainment

Revival blazes, even more, when destiny is awakened and released from the loins of people. As your team is trained and equipped, as revivals grows, they can assist in training and equipping others. As the region is infused with the presence and kingdom of God, heaven on earth becomes evident in your sphere of influence.

LABORING FOR REVIVAL

There have been times where revival awakens, the fire blazes, and people are too focused on the fire, they forget about the vision. If the vision of the fire is not fed and cultivated, the fire will go out. You have to feed a revival fire with more than just ministry events.

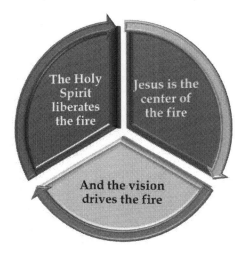

The vision cannot be neglected. No matter how much the glory blazes in services, people need to be trained, equipped, and released to ignite revival into the communities of the region. This is the reason team ministry is important. As everyone does their part in laboring for the vision, it makes it easier to remain fervent and consistent in bringing the full vision to past.

Do not be so quick to grow revival that you do not establish a solid foundation to build upon.

Ephesians 2:19-22 Now therefore ye are no more strangers and foreigners, but fellow citizens with the saints, and of

*the household of God; And are built upon the foundation of
the apostles and prophets, Jesus Christ himself being the
chief corner stone; In whom all the building fitly framed
together groweth unto an holy temple in the Lord: In whom
ye also are builded together for an habitation of God
through the Spirit.*

A SHIFT took place in this passage of scripture where the
people were transformed from church saints (strangers and
foreigners) to kingdom heirs (citizens). Fivefold ministry
was released, and Jesus dying and resurrecting, SHIFTED
him to being the head of the church, where apostles and
prophets could build his kingdom in the unity and maturity
of the faith. The foundation of all Jesus accomplished
through salvation was essential for the people and ministry
inhabiting God and his presence.

*John 3:16 For God so loved the world, that he gave his only
begotten Son, that whosoever believeth in him should not
perish, but have everlasting life. For God sent not his Son
into the world to condemn the world; but that the world
through him might be saved.*

The word "*save*" in the Greek is "*sozo*" and means:
1. to save, i.e., deliver or protect (literally or figuratively)
2. heal, preserve, save (self), do well, be (make) whole
3. to keep safe and sound, to rescue from danger or
   destruction, to deliver one (from injury or peril)
4. to save a suffering one (from perishing), i.e., one
   suffering from disease, to make well, heal, restore to
   health
5. to preserve one who is in danger of destruction, to save
   or rescue

If we are really saved – living on the chief cornerstone of
Jesus - then we should be living, expecting, cultivating, and

continuously pursuing the fullness of salvation. We should be delivered, protected, free from danger, death and destruction, healed, whole and journeying in the fullness of salvation. In order to awaken revival, we must build a solid foundation rooted in salvation so that the revival fire can sustain throughout generations. Building a solid foundation will require us to labor and contend for revival glory.

> *Jeremiah 1:10 See, I have this day set thee over the nations and over the kingdoms, to root out, and to pull down, and to destroy, and to throw down, to build, and to plant.*

With regional revival, there ought to be fervent, consist, lifestyle labor of:

- ➤ Rooting out - destroy, forsake, pluck (out, up, by the roots), pull up, utterly
- ➤ Pulling down - beat down, break down (out), cast down, destroy, overthrow, pull down, throw down.
- ➤ Destroying - to perish, to be undone, utterly, be void of, to kill, die, be exterminated
- ➤ Throwing down - overthrow, dismantle, crush, beat down, ruin utterly
- ➤ Building - to repair, build, rebuild, restore, establish, cause to continue, obtain children
- ➤ Planting - to strike in, to fix, to plant, to sow, to be planters, to establish

This word set is a governmental word. It is an ordination to a particular spiritual office in the kingdom of God, for the purpose of completing a work from his throne. You have been SET over your region by God to labor!

Oftentimes with revival, though we have times of repentance and cleansing, we neglect the implement of the first four mandates where we effectively govern over a region and ignite sustainable revival. The first four mandates need to be completed in the foundational stages of revival and are necessary for solidifying salvation and building a solid foundation for the revival fire to live upon. Depending on the principalities, curses, strongholds, and needs of your region, it could take years to successfully complete the first four where you have a solid foundation to build and plant upon revival fire.

Natural roots of a tree have been known to grow at least 20 feet deep in the ground. Some roots are ancient and have enmeshed with the soil and with each other, so it takes time to disconnect them and gut them out. For this reason, some trees and roots are cut to a stump then the stump is treated with chemicals that kill the roots. However, it still can take time for the stump and all its roots to die.

Pulling down insinuates that high places, imaginations, and materials have exalted themselves against God. Anything erected upward is usually constructed to be durable, so it can sustain against any atmospheric and physical contentions that would be a threat against it.

Destroy means to render unusable. Anything that is designed to be contrary to God and cannot be transformed into his likeness must be destroyed.

Building and planting is the reformation portion of revival that we discussed earlier in this book. These two mandates must be instituted so that the fashion of God can overtake people, the land, and the region. All six of these mandates require a lifestyle posture of revival.

> *Luke 10:2 And He said to them, The harvest indeed is abundant [there is much ripe grain], but the farmhands are*

few. Pray therefore the Lord of the harvest to send out laborers into His harvest.

There is plenty of harvest waiting for us as we do the work of the Lord, and there is a lot of people claiming to be workers of the Lord. But Jesus said the laborers are few. In the Greek, a *laborer* means, *"a toiler, a workman."*

Dictionary.com defines a *laborer "as a person engaged in work that requires bodily strength rather than skill or training."* It defines a *toilers* as, *"hard and continuous work, exhausting labor or effort, a laborious task, battle; strife, struggle."*

I believe these to be interesting definitions because in the body of Christ we rely heavily upon our skills and training and upon our gifts and callings. Both are essentials as we need to be skilled and trained and God has ordained it in his word. We must understand our giftings and callings in order to do the work of the Lord. But none of these spiritual wells can sustain us when there is a fervent work to be done. As a revivalist and revival ministries, it is important to understand that if this is what God is requiring of us, we have been anointed with the ability to toil. Hard work is a part of our lifestyle and purpose. It is not anything we are striving to receive.

- ❖ We must know we are mantled with it and operate through it.
- ❖ We cannot look at what God is calling us to do and say it is too much.
- ❖ We cannot allow hard work to steal the strength of our destiny to do the work.
- ❖ We cannot get discouraged or overwhelmed by hard work.

- ❖ We cannot build some religious false doctrine to try and get out of hard work as this short changes and stifles the vision that is in our hands.
- ❖ We cannot get upset when others appear to be doing nothing or seem to have the easy road, and we are continuously at war and work to complete the vision of the Lord.
- ❖ We cannot dread the work; we must love the work.
- ❖ We must be in love with working.
- ❖ We must get our thrills out of working for Jesus.
- ❖ We must pray for others with a laborer anointing to come along side us and tenaciously work.

Apostle John Eckhardt, a mighty prophetic and deliverance general of the faith, shared a revelation that there is a grace to work. That some have a greater grace to work than others. He gave this scripture reference to support his revelation:

> **1Corinthians 15:10** *But by the grace of God I am what I am, and his grace to me was not without effect. No, I worked harder than all of them--yet not I, but the grace of God that was with me.*

I was so blessed by that revelation because I am offended teased, ridiculed, envied, and questioned about how much I do and get done for God. I am often made to feel like I "*do too much,*" or that I sacrifice too much. But really the things I do are at the leading of the Lord. When I do not do them, when I do not remain in the momentum and flow of God, I become grieved and convicted in my spirit. What should be released through me becomes a burden upon me. I feel it demanding to be birthed forth. If I slack, I become even more burdened and overwhelmed, because then I am striving to catch up with myself, by birthing what I should have did last week, along with what I am being encouraged to do this week. I have learned that my strength and power reside in being at peace that this is my lifestyle mandate. I have had to learn to be at peace that I love producing for God, and I love laboring for him. It is the thrill of my life and where I find my most fulfillment. People do not understand it, and they do not have to. The revelation Apostle Eckhardt revealed helped me to understand that I have been graced by God to produce to this magnitude. It is who I am and who he is in me.

> *Revelation 4:7-8 The first of these living beings was like the lion, the second was like an ox; the third had a human; and the fourth was like an eagle in flight. And the four beasts had each of them six wings about him; and they were full of eyes within: and they rest not day and night, saying, Holy, holy, holy, Lord God Almighty, which was, and is, and is to come. God reigns & there is nothing the devil can do about it!*

Look at the dimension of worship the four beasts where given unto God. They were *full of eyes within*. The word *eyes* in this scripture means. *"vision, knowing, envy or jealous."* They were full of vision and knowing concerning who God was and what their purpose was. There jealousy for him made them fervent, as they did not rest or cease in saying "Holy, Holy, Holy!" Being *full of eyes* within denotes dimensions of God within them that could not be touched, stifled, or quenched. Such a depth in God fortified his laboring anointing within them. This is the life of the revivalists and revival ministries. They are seeking to constantly give God glory and to see God get glory. Their labor releases the reigns of the Lord, while annihilating the powers of the devil. He watches helplessly as your very identity, life, destiny, calling, ministry, and workings, reveals, unveils, and establishes God's glory in your sphere. **COME ON HERE JESUS! WHEWWW! SHIFT!**

We also discern from this passage of scripture that God was all around them and fortified who they were. They fortified the past, present, and future by declaring what they saw *"which was, and is, and is to come;"* and it became a shield of his glory and identity round about them. God is always holy, and there is nothing the devil can do about that. There is such POWERRRRR in this perspective. To cause revival, you must have His eyes of revival and labor from the fullness of his enlightenment within you.

> *Revelation 19:12 New Living Translation His eyes were like flames of fire, and on his head were many crowns. A name was written on him that no one understood except himself."*

WHEWWWW! SHIFT!

Okay, let us calm down and return to the *Jeremiah 1:10* scripture. The mandate definitions commands us to utterly root out, pull down, destroy, overthrow, build, and plant. This will require intense labor in the physical and natural realm of:

* ❖ Teaching
* ❖ Training
* ❖ Equipping
* ❖ Interceding
* ❖ Warring
* ❖ Contending
* ❖ Planting
* ❖ Plowing
* ❖ Building
* ❖ Establishing
* ❖ Maintaining
* ❖ Sustaining

You cannot do the spiritual work and hope the natural comes to pass. All of these laborious actions and whatever else God gives you will have to be done in the physical and the natural realm to see revival glory ignited in your region.

> **Matthew 6:10** *Thy kingdom come. Thy will be done in earth, as it is in heaven.*

> **Matthew 18:18** *I will give you the keys of the kingdom of heaven. Whatever you bind on earth will be bound in heaven, and whatever you loose on earth will be loosed in heaven.*

- ✓ You pray, then do, and God will manifest.
- ✓ You pray in every area regarding the laborious actions, then obey in igniting the vision, then God will manifest heaven in your earth.

Decreeing fresh laboring revival fire is overtaking you even now. **SHIFT!**

EVANGELIZING THE LOST

As you cultivate regional revival, it is important to seek God for strategies for how to draw the lost and unsaved. Many will come, but you are seeking to do a regional takeover, therefore, there will be some you have to go and get. The more people in the region are saved and are being cultivated in the revival glory, the greater the fire blazes, as the region is SHIFTED into the likeness of God's kingdom.

Word of the Lord to revivalists and the body of Christ as a whole (January 9, 2018):

You need to pray and pursue the most notorious sinners in your region to be saved because they operate as human, demonic principalities. When they are saved, it weakens the territorial spirits over the region and frees numerous people within the region to be drawn into salvation through revival fire. God says, "saints like to pick on the sick and the needy because they want to see miracles, signs, and wonders. But I want you to pick on the most notorious, so I can show you awe striking miracles, signs, and wonders."

"Though not all, some of the notorious are hidden in plain sight. You walk pass them in Walmart to go pick on that person in the wheelchair. Some are hidden for real. Pray for them to be exposed and pray for a revival fire that sends them bowing to their knees crying out to me. Pray to have favor where others would not be allowed close to them. But you will be invited to sit at the table with them and see my revival glory burn the devil out of their heart and soul. Yes, still pick on the sick and the lost, but go after the demonic principalities," says the Lord.

> **Matthew 9:10-13** *And as Jesus reclined at table in the house, behold, many tax collectors and [especially wicked]*

239

sinners came and sat (reclined) with Him and His disciples. And when the Pharisees saw this, they said to His disciples, Why does your Master eat with tax collectors and those [preeminently] sinful?

But when Jesus heard it, He replied, Those who are strong and well (healthy) have no need of a physician, but those who are weak and sick. Go and learn what this means: I desire mercy [that is, readiness to help those in trouble] and not sacrifice and sacrificial victims. For I came not to call and invite [to repentance] the righteous (those who are upright and in right standing with God), but sinners (the erring ones and all those not free from sin).

I shared this word with my team, and Minister Mercedes Carr said: *"That is when you know you really have the keys to the gates; when God starts unlocking and revealing the unsearchable things to you. Not everybody can do that kind of work."*

This quickened me to understand that regional gatekeepers must contend with physical principalities as well spiritual principalities, and when they do, it unlocks deliverance for massive breakthrough.

> **Mark 3:27** *The Amplified Bible But no one can go into a strong man's house and ransack his household goods right and left and seize them as plunder unless he first binds the strong man; then indeed he may [thoroughly] plunder his house.*

This dimension of evangelism denotes a seizing as plunder. Seize the human principality and plunder his house. Multitudes are saved, and the devil house is depleted.

Word of the Lord to revivalists and the body of Christ as a whole (January 10, 2018):

I hear the Lord saying that cancer and other incurable diseases and disorders such as autism, ALS, Multiple sclerosis, Parkinson's Disease, Diabetes, HIV/AIDS, deformities, illnesses, and mental alternations due to vaccinations, have become demonic principalities. Go after them as principalities. Strong arm them and their powers.

Mental illness, suicide, terrorist attacks, LGBTQ community (lesbian, gay, bisexual, and transgender, questioning) are principalities. Many bound under these principalities have become human principalities in the earth or are overtaken by the regional principalities within their sphere of influence. Go after the principalities says the Lord. Strong arm them and their powers.

Asthma, bone and join disorders, stomach issues, immune disorders, thyroid problems have become common place incurable diseases due to pollution in the land and deterioration of food production. These are principalities of death and hell are governing over agriculture and Food and Drug Administration. As you pray for people, pray for these principalities - these demonic kingdoms - to fall down, otherwise people will just keep getting ill. Be fervent in praying over your food and your water says the Lord and detaching yourself from principalities governing these realms. My kingdom people, as you seek to rule in the market place and regions, commit to building your own stores and growing your own crops. Take back your right to own the land, be healthy and to distribute health to others. Know that I will bless your land and your bread and your water.

> **Exodus 23:25** *And ye shall serve the LORD your God, and he shall bless thy bread, and thy water; and I will take sickness away from the midst of thee.*

"Many of you are full of my power - greater works are upon and evident in you. The reason you are not seeing consistent miracles when you pray for people is that you are going after foot soldier demons. You must go after territorial spirits and principalities. The strongman must be seized. It must be seized in people's lives, in the land, and in regions. You have my power; you must assert authority in the correct sphere. The sphere of seated in me in heavenly places. You want revival and reformation; you must combat the big boys says the Lord. You got big power - limitless power. You have contended for it. Think higher. Come up higher. And crush and displaced principalities for my glory. For I hear some of you saying, *"but that is not my jurisdiction."* **Who told you that? Who fed you lies? It was the father of lies, disguised as a religious guide. I say come up higher to crush the darkness in this hour." says the Lord.**

> *Ephesians 6:12 says, For we wrestle not against flesh and blood, but against principalities, against powers, against the rulers of the darkness of this world, against spiritual wickedness in high places.*

That is my word, and your truth says the Lord.

> *John 14-12:14 The Amplified Bible I assure you, most solemnly I tell you, if anyone steadfastly believes in Me, he will himself be able to do the things that I do; and he will do even greater things than these, because I go to the Father. And I will do [I Myself will grant] whatever you ask in My Name [as presenting all that I AM], so that the Father may be glorified and extolled in (through) the Son. [Yes] I will grant [I Myself will do for you] whatever you shall ask in My Name [as presenting all that I AM].*

You go after these principalities in your private time and with your intercessory prayer teams, so when you pray for people, you will be in a position of authority and have already broken the powers of principalities and territorial spirits off of them. You may have to confront them when praying for people. BE BOLD AND CONFRONT SAYS THE LORD. This is the season of being bold. While you are trying to be politically religiously correct, the enemy is being bold, and devouring says the Lord. SHIFT!

BIRTHING REVIVAL CHEAT SHEET

- Revival begins with personal revival within people who want the fullness of salvation manifested in every area of their lives.
- Revival requires continual fervent prayer, intercession, and warfare for the region and the people.
- The Holy Spirit must be free to operate as revival fire. Revivalists and team members, must have a personal relationship with the Holy Spirit and understand that the Holy Spirit must have free reign if revival is going to be sustained in a region.
- Revival requires a consistent cultivating of the glory of God such that his presence and open heaven reign over the people, communities, and the region.
- The fallow ground of the land and regions must be broken up and cultivated so that the kingdom of God can infuse the land, and transform it to the likeness of heaven.
- Exalting Jesus is essential to establishing revival. It is important to be specific about who God is and declaring him above every other name and idol god.
- The art of liberated worship provokes, unveils, and establish revival in a people and regions. Real praise and worship that exudes the hunger of God and demonstrates that the people, land, and region is surrendered in abandoned worship unto God must be evident. Teaching people how to praise and worship freely is necessary for revival to remain ablaze in people and regions.
- Prophetic spiritual songs and decrees that are in alignment with the vision of revival and specific events that are utilized annihilating the spirit of death, while cultivating revival and the "newness" and "new things" of God.

- Fine Arts Ministry is essential to revival. Fine Arts Ministries demonstrate the creativity, uniqueness, and liberation of God. These ministers are essential to being examples of utilizing their gifts and mantles to worship, war, intercede, and contend for revival in abandonment.
- Dance ministers are essential to breaking up the fallow ground, maintaining the territory that has been taken up in people's lives, the land, atmospheres, climates, and regions.
- Living in supernatural realms and continually pursuing a higher and deeper dimension in the glory of the Lord will continuously stir and blaze revival. Never settling or become complacent in an experience or movement. Seeking God to build upon each moment and experience will keep revival progressing and advancing in people and regions.
- People and the region must live through a posture of expectation, where they hunger and desire for the presence, will, and purpose of God.
- Repentance must be active in the lives of the revivalists and within the ministries that are trailblazing revival. Constant repentance of the sins of the people, land, and generations is essential for breaking personal, generational, community, and regional curses and strongholds, and displacing principalities and powers.
- Cleansing witchcraft from the land, tearing down high places, and judging witches and warlocks is essential to purifying the region and solidifying the glory of God in the region.
- Recognizing that as revival blaze, sinners and those that need deliverance and healing will be drawn to the ministry is very important, as witchcraft that is stirred up from the land, region, other spheres of influence and from the people, will constantly need to be repented for and cleansed from the atmosphere. Otherwise, your

worship unto Lord and atmosphere is mixed with strange fire. Strange fire quenches and hinders the fullness of revival fire from operating. Or people are being contaminated with strange fire even as they are receiving purified revival fire.

- Principalities and territorial spirits will not just give up the people and region freely. Learning the strongholds of the people, land, and region, learning spiritual warfare, and understanding that combating strongholds is a part of your calling is essential to displacing principalities and powers within the region.

- Gatekeeping Intercession needs to be ever present. Revivalists must make regional intercession a part of their everyday prayer time, while continuously guarding the gates of the region for the glory of God.

- Training, equipping and releasing people into their destiny and life's vision is essential to taking over the region and sustaining regional revival. There must be a mindset to infiltrate the region with businesses, stores, schools, entertainment, social service agencies, political mandates, and mindsets, etc. This reformation is essential to the world being drawn to God and his kingdom rather than the saints relying on the world's kingdom to cultivate their life and destiny. This is also essential for the region SHIFTING into the likeness of God's kingdom, where his governmental rule is evident and eternal.

- Gathering believers from different ministries to help ignite revival is vital to truly establishing and sustaining revival in the region. Please understand that there has to be some commonality in your biblical beliefs and you must be on one accord on how to birth revival. Otherwise, your revival foundation will be unstable, and you open the door for constant discord, division, and disruption of revival advance in your midst.

- Drawing the lost is essential for revival. Once you ignite and sustain the fire, implementing a strategic plan of evangelism is necessary for further transforming people and the region into the likeness of God. The more souls are saved, the more contagious the revival fire is, where it spreads to other spheres of influence.

- Guarding your altar is important to revival fire. It is vital to have altar workers, watchman, and catchers on alert to make sure the altar remains safe where people will not get hurt from falling, and where they are receiving deliverance and healing from those who are an approved part of the ministry. Witches, warlocks, the demonized, kooky people, and opportunists love to lurk around revival and contaminate the altar of God with strange fire.

- God gives apostolic grace and a fivefold ministry TEAM mandate to laboring for revival. Revival is not an event; it is a lifestyle. Revival must become the essence of the revivalist's, the team's, and ministries' identity, such that they are able to sustain in the progress, advancement, and establishment of the kingdom of God reigning in their sphere of influence.

VISION PLAN FOR IGNITING REVIVAL

When you have a clear vision plan, it is easier to acquire further strategy and revelation from God as you seek to ignite revival.

> **Proverbs 29:18** *Where there is no vision, the people perish: but he that keepeth the law, happy is he.*
>
> **New International Version** *Where there is no revelation, people cast off restraint; but blessed is the one who heeds wisdom's instruction.*
>
> **New Living Translation** *When people do not accept divine guidance, they run wild. But whoever obeys the law is joyful.*

Vision is *hâzôn* in the Hebrew and means, *"a sight (mentally), i.e., a dream, revelation, or oracle (divine communication or wisdom), divine prophecy."*

Revival activation questions to examine before the Lord. Journal what he says to you can make the vision plan in the earth.

- What is your destiny and life's calling?
- What are the ministries, businesses, and other endeavors God has called you to release in the earth?
- What is significant regarding your destiny right now where you feel it is essential to launching regional revival?
- What is God speaking concerning revival in your region?
- How will you balance your time to work on the vision of revival and maintain in your other endeavors in your life?

- Ask God to reveal to you at least five people in your personal circle who you can immediately partner with to ignite revival. Ask God what ministries or people within the region with like spirits that can assist you with the vision. Ask God what each person's purpose to your revival vision. Journal what he shares with you. Ask him for a specific time of release for discussing the vision with them. Be obedient to what he says. When you share the vision with them, give them some time to pray into it, and get back with you on what God speaks to them regarding the revival and their role in assisting with revival.
- Considering each category within your region; journal the bondages in the
  - People
  - Land
  - Ministries in the region
  - The economic system
  - Atmosphere
  - Climate
  - Heavenlies
  - Region as a whole
- Ask God to reveal the principalities and powers in the region. Ask him to identify two that you need to begin combating as you launch your vision.
- Even if you have a prayer team in your ministry, identify five strong apostolic intercessors that can consistently soak the revival in prayer, and assist with other prayer needs.
- As God to identity fivefold ministry officers within the region that can help you guard the gates and contend for regional revival.
- Ask God for revelation of how and when to launch the revival vision.

- Ask God what trainings you and those helping you need to strengthen your revival mantles. Implement what he says immediately. Do not allow the work of the revival override training. They should go hand in hand to equip you in effectively igniting revival.
- Seek God consistently for continual strategies for planting, plowing, building, and solidifying revival in your region.
- Refer to this book consistently to receive strategy and revelation regarding igniting revival in your region. You got this! GO FORTH! SHIFT!

APPENDIX

A Brief History of Spiritual Revival and Awakening in America By Patrick Morley

June 30, 2015

In describing what happened in **Jonathan Edward's** Northampton, Massachusetts church in 1734, observers said, "It pleased God...to display his free and sovereign mercy in the conversion of a great multitude of souls in a short space of time, turning them from a formal, cold, and careless profession of Christianity, to the lively exercise of every Christian grace, and the powerful practice of our holy religion."

That's about as clear a definition as we'll ever get! During a revival, God supernaturally transforms believers and non-believers in a church, locale, region, nation, or the world through sudden, intense enthusiasm for Christianity. People sense the presence of God powerfully; conviction, despair, contrition, repentance, and prayer come easily; people thirst for God's word; many authentic conversions occur, and backsliders are renewed.

Revival and awakening are, generally, synonyms. The larger the geography a revival covers, the greater the tendency to call it an awakening.

America has a deep, rich history of revivals and awakenings.

Revivals in America: A Well-Travelled Road

The Great Awakening, 1734-43. In December 1734, the first revival of historic significance broke out in Northampton, Massachusetts, where a young **Jonathan Edwards** was

251

pastor. After months of fruitless labor, he reported five or six people converted--one a young woman. He wrote, "[She] had been one of the greatest company-keepers in the whole town." He feared her conversion would douse the flame, but quite the opposite took place. Three hundred souls converted in six months--in a town of only 1,100 people! The news spread like wildfire, and similar revivals broke out in over 100 towns. Starting in Philadelphia in 1739, **George Whitfield's** dramatic preaching was like striking a match to the already-underway awakening. An estimated 80% of America's 900,000 Colonists personally heard Whitfield preach. He became America's first celebrity.

The Second Great Awakening, 1800-1840. In 1800, only one in 15 of America's population of 5,300,000 belonged to an evangelical church. Presbyterian minister **James McGready** presided over strange spiritual manifestations in Logan County, Kentucky. The resulting camp meeting revivals drew thousands from as far away as Ohio. Rev. Gardiner Spring reported that for the next 25 years not a single month passed without news of a revival somewhere. In 1824, **Charles Finney** began a career that would eventually convert 500,000 to Christ. An unparalleled 100,000 were converted in Rochester, New York, in 1831 alone--causing the revival to spread to 1,500 towns. By 1850 the nation's population exploded fourfold to 23,000,000 people, but those connected to evangelical churches grew nearly tenfold from 7% to 13% of the population--from 350,000 to 3,000,000 church members!

The Businessmen's Revival of 1857-1858. In 1857, the North Dutch Church in New York City hired a businessman, **Jeremiah Lanphier**, to be a lay missionary. He prayed, "Lord, what would you have me do?" Concerned by the anxious faces of businessmen on the streets of New York City, Lanphier decided to open the church at noon so businessmen could pray. The first meeting was set for September 23--three weeks before the Bank Panic of 1857. Six attended the first week, 20 the next, then 40, then they switched to daily meetings. Before long all the space was taken, and other churches also began to open up for businessmen's prayer meetings. 15 Revivals broke out everywhere in 1857, spreading throughout the United States and world. Sometimes called **The Great Prayer Meeting Revival**, an estimated 1,000,000 people were added to America's church rolls, and as many as 1,000,000 of the 4,000,000 existing church members also converted.

The Civil War Revival, 1861-1865. The bitter dispute over slavery thrust our nation into the deadliest war we've ever experienced. By the end, 620,000 Americans lay dead--one out of every 50 of the 31,000,000 people counted in the 1860 census. At the start of the Civil War in 1861, it seemed as though the soldiers for both sides had left their Christianity at home and gone morally berserk. By 1862, the tide turned, first among the Confederate forces. An estimated 300,000 soldiers were converted, evenly divided between the Southern and Northern Armies.

The Urban Revivals, 1875-1885. Young businessman **Dwight L. Moody** participated in the Great Revival of 1857 as it swept Chicago. Moody later conducted revivals throughout the British Isles where he spoke to more than 2,500,000 people. In 1875, Moody returned home and began revivals in America's biggest cities. Hundreds of thousands were converted, and millions were inspired by the greatest soul winner of his generation. At this time, the general worldview of Americans was shifting away from a Christian consensus. Darwinism and higher criticism were gaining traction, and Moody became the first evangelist to come under attack--accused of making religion the opiate of the masses.21

By the turn of the twentieth century, the mood of the country was changing. Outside the church, it was the era of radio, movies, and the "Jazz Age." World War I led to a moral letdown and the Roaring Twenties. When that era came to an abrupt end on October 29, 1929, followed by the Great Depression, there was surprisingly little interest in spiritual revival. Inside the church, a half-century long battle raged between evangelicalism and theological liberalism which had penetrated major denominations. The effect was that twentieth century revivals were more limited in scope, and lacked the broad impact on society of earlier awakenings.

The Revivals of 1905-1906. Word of the **Welsh Revival of 1904-1905** spread to Welsh-speaking settlers in Pennsylvania in late 1904 and revival broke out. By 1905, local revivals blazed in places like Brooklyn, Michigan, Denver, Schenectady, Nebraska, North and South Carolina, Georgia, Taylor University, Yale University, and Asbury College in Wilmore, Kentucky. **Billy Sunday**, who became a key figure about this time, preached to more than 100,000,000 people with an estimated 1,000,000 or more conversions.

The Azusa Street Revival, 1906. In 1906, **William J. Seymour**, an African-American Holiness pastor blind in one eye, went to Los Angeles to be candidate for a pastoral job. But after he preached, he was locked out of the second service! He began prayer meetings in a nearby home and the Spirit of God, which they called "the second blessing," fell after many months of concerted prayer. Eventually, the interracial crowds became so large they acquired a dilapidated Methodist church at 312 Azusa Street where daily meetings continued for three years. The resulting **Pentecostal Movement** and the later **Charismatic Movement**, which both exploded worldwide in the twentieth century both trace their roots to this revival. **The**

Post-World War II Awakening. After World War II, in 1947 and 1948, Pentecostals experienced two strands of awakening, one the **Latter Rain Revival** and the other **the Healing Revival**. Large numbers of evangelicals also experienced revival resulting in many conversions. It was at this time that a great generation of Christian leaders emerged. **Bill Bright** began Campus Crusade for Christ. In 1949, **Billy Graham's** distinguished career, which popularized evangelical Christianity for a new generation, exploded on the scene during his Los Angeles crusade sponsored by the **Christian Businessmen's Committee**. An estimated 180,000,000 people attended his nearly 400 crusades, and millions more viewed on television. **College Revivals** started as early as 1946, but when the prayer-based **Wheaton College Revival of 1950** achieved national publicity, it sparked other college revivals throughout America.

The Charismatic Renewal and Jesus Movement. During the late 1960s and early 1970s more revivals of national scope developed. The first strand was the **Charismatic Renewal** which spread far beyond Pentecostal and Holiness churches to college campuses, the Catholic Church, and mainline denominations. The second strand, the widely publicized **Jesus Movement**, emphasized turning from drugs, sex, and radical politics to taking the Bible at face value and finding Jesus Christ as personal Savior. Not surprisingly, this revival spread to college campuses, most notably the **1970 Asbury College Revival** in Wilmore, Kentucky. Within a week the revival had spread throughout the entire country. In 1976 America elected a born-again president, and evangelicalism has continued to prosper from then to now.

The Mid-1990s Revivals. Despite the widespread secularization of society since the Cultural Revolution that began in the late 1960s, in the mid-1990s God once again brought a series of revivals, mostly to Charismatic and Pentecostal groups. In 1994 it was **The Toronto Blessing,** and 1995 ushered in the **Melbourne Revival** on Florida's Space Coast, the **Modesto Revival,** and the **Brownsville Revival** in Pensacola, Florida, which recorded 100,000 conversions in two years. College Revivals swept across America, starting at Howard Payne University in Brownwood, Texas, under the preaching of **Henry Blackaby,** a Southern Baptist.

The Promise Keepers Revival, the most publicized of the mid-1990s Revivals, began in 1991 when 4,200 men descended on the University of Colorado to be challenged to live up to their faith. In 1993, 50,000 men assembled from every state and 16 nations. In the following years, stadium events were conducted in cities throughout the United States. A spirit of revival and transformation swept across America as millions of men attended. The revival reached its zenith on October 4, 1997, as 1,000,000 or more men gathered on the National Mall in Washington, D.C. By the close of 2000, Promise Keepers reported 5,000,000 had attended 100 conferences. An additional 1,000,000 men have been impacted since.

Ten Characteristics of Revivals

Each revival or awakening leaves its own heat signature; in 1740 youth led the way, in 1857 businessmen and prayer took center stage, and the 1906 Azusa Street revival was decidedly interracial. Yet all share common themes. What are the most frequently mentioned characteristics of revivals and awakenings in literature?

1. **TIMING:** Revivals emerge during times of spiritual and moral decline, which leads to intense prayer.

2. **PRAYER:** God puts a longing into the hearts of many to pray for revival.
3. **THE WORD:** The preaching or reading of God's Word brings deep conviction and desire for Christ.
4. **THE HOLY SPIRIT:** The Holy Spirit takes people to a spiritual depth they could not achieve on their own.
5. **CONVICTION:** Affected sinners are inconsolable except in Christ.
6. **GLORY FOR GOD**: God receives praise, honor, and glory for bringing revival.
7. **REFORMATION AND RENEWAL:** Revival produces lasting fruit. New ministries are founded, and society experiences a reform of morals as more and more people convert.
8. **MANIFESTATIONS:** Manifestations like fainting, groaning prayer, and miracles vary by culture and denomination.
9. **MESSY:** Revivals are messy--controversies swirl about miracles, abuses, excesses, suspicions, and theological disputes (to name but a few).
10. **CYCLICAL:** Revivals inevitably crest and decline.

BOOK REFERENCES

- *A Brief History of Spiritual Revival and Awakening in America by Patrick Morley*

- *Apostolic Mantle by Taquetta Baker*

- *Blueletterbible.com*

- *Biblestudytools.com*

- *Dictionary.com*

- *Dry land image is from https://yessweeterthanhoney.wordpress.com/2012/07/13/thirst-for-the-lord-today/*

- *God's Shifter Power by Taquetta Baker*

- *Olivetree.com*

- *Circle of Incantations Picture is from https://www.tumblr.com/search/circles%20of%20incantations*

- *Strong's Exhaustive Bible Concordance Online Bible Study Tools*

- *Sustaining The Vision Workbook by Taquetta Baker*

- *The Golden Garments (8th) of The Kohen Gadol Shemot 28:4:42 is from http://www.british-israel.us/185.html*

- *The High Priest Golden Garment Picture is from <u>http://narrowgateentrance.com/priest-garments/</u>*

- *The High Priest's Garment Picture is from <u>http://www.british-israel.us/185.html</u>*

- *Vestment Picture is from <u>http://www.british-israel.us/185.html</u>*

- *Wikipedia*

  - *Front Book cover photo by Tashema Davis. Connect with her via Facebook.*

  - *Cover photo by Reenita Keys. Connect with her via Facebook.*

  - *Editing by Amanda Latrice. Connect with her via Facebook.*

Kingdom Shifters Books & Apparel

Available at <u>Kingdomshifters.com</u>

Made in the USA
Columbia, SC
08 February 2018